The Horse on the Balcony

The Horse on the Balcony

Jane Ayres

The Horse on the Balcony
Copyright: © 2008 by Jane Ayres
Cover and interior illustrations: © Jennifer Bell
Cover layout: Stabenfeldt A/S
Typeset by Roberta L. Melzl
Editor: Bobbie Chase
Printed in Germany, 2009

ISBN: 978-1-934983-08-9

Stabenfeldt, Inc.
225 Park Avenue South
New York, NY 10003
www.pony4kids.com

Available exclusively through PONY.

Chapter 1

It was like any other day.

Jenni woke, as always, when her radio alarm went off at precisely 7 a.m. Although it was a Saturday, with no school to worry about, Jenni still got up early so she could spend as much time as possible with Smokey. It was important, she told herself, to keep a regular routine, because horses liked routine. They needed to know that everything was as it should be, that nothing was about to change. No surprises. Horses hated surprises, and she couldn't blame them for that.

Jenni remembered the birthday surprise her older brother, Az, had arranged for her almost a year ago when he was on army leave and was supposed to be taking care of her while their parents were away on vacation. He'd whisked her off to the countryside in his four-wheel drive, for a day out.

"Wear jeans," he'd said. "And a scruffy jacket, because you might get a little muddy outdoors."

She'd had misgivings even before she'd spotted the sign to the Outdoor Adventure Center. Then they were handed their equipment and harness, and the instructor said, "Have you ever been rappelling before?" Her stomach lurched as she peered over the edge of the rock wall.

"You *know* I'm terrified of heights, Az!"

"Yeah. It's just a phobia. So this will help you get over it, sis. Don't be such a baby."

"I can't do it," she replied.

"Yes, you can. There's no such word as 'can't'. Anyway, I've already paid for it – it's my birthday treat. I'll be upset if you don't even try." He'd gone first, to show her how easy it was, and then stood at the bottom, waiting for her.

So she took several deep breaths, pressed her eyes tightly shut, trembling and shaking as her feet bounced off the side of the fiberglass boulder. At the bottom Jenni promptly threw up all over Az's brand new hiking boots.

This year, Jenni would be fourteen in a few weeks, and she had already decided how she was going to celebrate. Pulling on her T-shirt and navy jodhpurs, she pictured herself riding her iron gray gelding down the trail by the woods, just the two of them, and stopping by the river at one of their favorite spots to watch the heron and egrets on the water, and the little kingfisher bird that hunted there. It would be a sunny day, warm and calm, and they would spend the whole day together, just riding and walking and sitting, until finally the sky turned dark and she would come home and put Smokey to bed in the stable. She would brush his soft coat until it shone and make sure he had fresh hay and water before she finally, reluctantly, kissed him goodnight.

They had been together half of her life. She was seven when her parents had finally agreed, after endless pleading, to buy her a pony. She tried three other ponies, all nice in their own ways, from answering ads in the local paper, but none of them were quite what she wanted.

Then her mom had taken her to the Summer Open Day at the local animal rescue center. Smokey was on his own in a little paddock, looking forlorn and lost while the other horses and donkeys gathered eagerly at the gate, hoping for attention. He looked thin and small somehow, even though he was just over 14 hands high. His head hung low, dejected, and his gun-metal gray mane and tail were wispy and uneven.

"He hasn't been here long, poor thing," one of the helpers told them. "Cruelty case. Goodness knows what he went through. When we were alerted, he was half starved, riddled with worms and he'd rubbed his mane nearly raw. But he's making a good recovery and he is really sweet-natured."

She'd wanted to take him home then and there, to love and protect him, but she'd had to be patient, wait until he was completely fit and healthy, and then wait some more as her family were checked out and found to be suitable and responsible people.

She'd learned to ride when she was four, and spent all her spare time at the local stables learning everything she could about ponies. Their house was out of town, and there was a nice big field just across the road, which was owned by a horse-loving neighbor whose daughter kept her pony there. So Smokey would have company and lots of attention.

For the first week after they brought him home, Jenni couldn't stop gazing at him through her bedroom window, where she had a perfect view of the field. He was the first thing she saw when she woke up in the morning. Eight years later, she felt exactly the same about Smokey. She had never felt such love for anyone or anything in her life.

"Don't be home late for lunch, love," said her mom as Jenni grabbed an apple from the kitchen fruit bowl to give to Smokey as a treat.

"I'll try not to," Jenni grinned. "But you know how I lose track of time when I'm out riding."

"Yes. I do know. Sometimes I think you love that pony too much."

Jenni laughed. "What an odd thing to say. You can't possibly love *too* much."

She dashed outside into the warm summer air, her boots crunching on the gravel drive. She could see Smokey already standing at the gate, waiting for her as she crossed the quiet road. He tossed his head impatiently and whickered a gentle, comforting sound that still made Jenni feel warm inside when she heard it.

"Hello, baby," she murmured, rubbing her face against his silky soft muzzle, his whiskers tickling her chin. He crunched the apple, slobbering on her hands. She vaulted over the gate and he followed her as she strolled across to the little locked shed that stored the feed, tack and grooming kit. He stood patiently as she began to brush off any dust and loose mud from his coat, both pony and girl enjoying the grooming ritual which bonded them. She picked out his hooves, cleaned the hoof pick and brushes and was already tacking up when a familiar voice shouted, "Hi, Jenni. You beat me to it again."

It was Ella, her neighbor's daughter and, besides Smokey, Jenni's best friend. Her cropped hair was standing up on end, like she had just gotten out of bed – which she had.

"Why don't you set your alarm if you want to get up early?" suggested Jenni for the hundredth time.

"On a Saturday? You've got be kidding. Besides, I'd probably sleep through it anyway. You know how I am." remarked Ella.

"I should by now. I'm going up past the woods and by the river. Do you want me to wait for you?"

"Depends on how long it takes me to catch Dylan. He's not like Smokey, coming when you call."

Dylan was Ella's new pony, which she'd only had for two weeks. He was a bright showy bay, young and badly schooled. Very unlike Mac, her last pony, which was steady, although a little bit of a plodder, or Darcy, her first pony, a perfect gentleman.

Ella liked to change her ponies to "upgrade," as she called it. She was like some people with cars or cell phones, reflected Jenni. Still, Ella had loved all of them, but she was ambitious and eager to "move up" in the competitive riding world, and she had high hopes for Dylan, who she claimed had lots of potential. If she could teach him some manners.

Jenni watched with interest while Ella made a number of attempts to catch Dylan, who was more concerned with munching grass than being caught. He successfully evaded Ella's maneuvers and although she nearly managed to grab his head collar a couple of times, he pulled away and trotted out of reach, his tail swishing naughtily. "This is going to take forever," admitted Ella wearily.

"Should I help?" offered Jenni, feeling a little guilty that she had never had this trouble with Smokey – not ever.

"Thanks, but I think two people chasing him will just be double the fun for the little devil. I'll have to resort to more devious measures."

"The bucket of pony nuts?"

"Correct."

"Mind if I go without you? I have to be back in time for lunch today."

"No problem. I'll catch up to you later. I know the route. I'll skip the river and probably meet you on the green."

"Okay."

Jenni swung into the saddle and Smokey moved off

amiably at a steady walk. The sun was high and warm.
Jenni watched affectionately as Smokey's ears flicked
back and forth in response to the twittering of the birds
in the hedges that lined their path. They had a brief
canter on the approach to the woods and then slowed
back to a trot, as Jenni had to duck the overhanging
brambles at the mouth of the little wooded glade. It was
like a private sanctuary, the tall trees forming a curved
roof, only letting in splinters of sunlight. Jenni loved the
quiet and solitude of the woods, the smell of the damp
earth underfoot. It was like the trees were some kind of
benevolent sentinel, making sure no harm came to her or
her pony as she passed through.

Wanting to savor its tranquility, Jenni reined in for a
moment, to listen to the silence. Smokey didn't fidget
once as some ponies might have and Jenni reflected that
they shared a special bond. It was as if they were able to
read each other's thoughts, or at least sense their mutual
moods. But she had connected with Smokey from Day
One, when she had approached that withdrawn creature
at the Animal Rescue Center, his eyes blank, as if he
had given up on the world around him. She'd held out
her hand to him, and let him smell her to see that she
meant no harm. She'd felt his warm breath on her palm,
her heart thumping as fast as his. Then he'd lifted his
head to look at her, really look at her, and he took a step

forward. She too had taken a step forward to match his. Then her hand was on his neck and he'd let her stroke him, reassure him. She'd felt his weight shift as he leaned against her hand, accepting her offer of help. From then on, there had been complete trust, and they had an unspoken agreement to protect each other.

A gentle breeze rustled the branches and Jenni knew they had to move on if she was to have time to go by the river.

The water was still, its surface lit by sparkles of sunlight and she smiled at the black and white coots and red beaked moorhens bobbing past. She got to see her kingfisher too, a flash of blue-green feathers diving before resurfacing and disappearing into the bushes. As she gazed, half day dreaming, Jenni suddenly felt a chill as a dark cloud passed across the sun. It hovered, blocking out the light before moving on again, but Jenni wondered if they were in for a sudden summer storm.

"Come on, Smokey, let's go for a gallop before turning back," she said, nudging his sides with her legs. She reveled in the thrill of speed as his hooves drummed on the grass, and her long honey blonde hair blew across her face so she had to shake her head to push it out of her eyes. Her fingers entwined in his wiry gray mane, she reflected, as she often did, on how lucky she was to have a pony like Smokey.

They were both panting when she pulled up, and she intended to walk the rest of the way back to cool off. But a quick glance at her watch informed her that it was already twelve thirty and she would be late for lunch. She didn't want to rush and end up with Smokey arriving home lathered, so she decided to take a shortcut down one of the many country lanes instead. It was a narrow road but open on both sides, so drivers would have good visibility and plenty of time to slow down for a pony and rider. Even so, for some reason, Smokey was reluctant to take this route.

"Hey, boy, what's the problem?" she murmured, increasing the pressure with her legs. "We've been this way before, I'm sure."

She pushed him into a trot but he still seemed agitated. Then she saw Ella in the distance, riding toward her across the farmland.

"So that's it, you saw Ella and Dylan." Jenni lifted one arm and gave a big wave to Ella at the very moment a car rounded the bend. In what must have been a split second, Jenni registered that the driver had taken the corner much too fast, and although he must have seen her, the car was skidding out of control and heading straight for them!

When Jenni regained consciousness minutes later, she was lying on a grassy bank next to the road. At first she couldn't see anything at all and her head throbbed hard, like someone was hitting it with a hammer – from the inside. There was a strange smell and she was aware of someone crying and glass crunching. She dragged herself up to a half sitting position and tried to stand, but when she put pressure on her right leg it felt as if someone had thrust a red-hot poker into it. She screamed with pain.

"I'm sorry. We didn't mean to. It was an accident."

She didn't know the voice but when she looked up, her vision still blurred, she could make out a boy. He was not much older than she, standing helplessly in the middle of the road, a huge red gash across his forehead. He looked terrified. She shifted her focus and noticed a car, its hood completely crumpled, windscreen shattered, another boy slumped forwards, not moving. Then she saw Smokey.

"It was an accident," the boy repeated, before he turned on his heels and ran.

The gray pony lay on his side. He wasn't moving. Jenni stopped the scream welling up in her chest as she crawled toward him, her nails scraping the concrete, her heart pounding violently. As she reached him, she saw that his coat was matted with sweat and blood, but he was still breathing. Just barely.

"Smokey," she breathed, the words catching like barbed wire in her throat. She reached out, touching his face with her badly grazed hands, her blood mingling with his. His eyes were open but glassy and filmed, as if he were no longer in this world. Did he know she was there?

"Please," she begged, tears trickling down her bruised face, the salt stinging her cut lip.

His breathing was labored, harsh and rasping.

She was aware of Ella's voice, somewhere behind her, muttering, "Oh no, oh no," but it was in the background, peripheral noise, because Jenni was completely focused on Smokey's breathing, which seemed to be getting slower. And slower. She was watching his life ebb away.

"Hold on, *please*, Smokey," she pleaded, her voice breaking. But his breathing got slower and the rasping got louder. A terrible, bone-chilling sound pierced her heart like a knife.

And then it stopped. And although Ella was sobbing uncontrollably and sirens were blaring, all Jenni could hear was the echoing silence.

Chapter 2

Holly gazed out of the window as the landscape outside rushed past in a rhythmic movement. She liked train journeys. She found them reassuring somehow, peaceful. Nice to be going somewhere, moving while having the luxury of time to think and reflect. She did a lot of that.

It was usually quiet when she got on the train at the little town where she lived with her father and sister. It chugged along, reaching the next stop only minutes later. Then, a horde of passengers boarded and she usually had to share her seat with businessmen and commuters. At least she got to sit near the window, watching the trees and fields as it pulled into open country. She was lucky to have this vacation job for the summer in the coffee bar of a bookstore. She liked books, loved reading, and enjoyed meeting people. The pay was OK, nothing special, but for five days a week she got away from the house and escaped from home life.

Even thinking that made her feel guilty again. It sounded so awful, when she had a nice home. Her Dad loved her – she knew he really did, even if he didn't always show it – and a twelve-year-old sister she was devoted to. She was lucky. Very lucky, compared to her sister, Claire. She sighed and stared fixedly at the changing landscape. Houses dotted the scenery now, and only two more stops down the line, the greenery would be replaced by office blocks, warehouses, and high-rise apartments.

Sometimes, she found it hard to remember life before the accident. Other times, the memories flashed back, crystal clear. Like coming home from school and seeing her mother making her favorite strawberry milkshake while Claire played happily on the kitchen floor with her latest toys. Or the whole family watching TV together in their comfy family room, with Claire playing happily on her Dad's lap while she was snuggled up next to her mom on the sofa. It all seemed like a long time ago. Holly missed her mom so much.

Before the accident Holly had been a real TV addict, watching anything and everything. Maybe it was an escape for her, although she couldn't imagine what she had to escape from. They were a happy family. Now, she hated the television and couldn't bear to even look at it.

The train was nearly there, only one more stop. She saw a group of horses grazing peacefully in a paddock, a girl riding in the next field, practicing over some homemade jumps. Her sister, Claire, loved ponies. She had been a talented rider, and for the first few years after the accident she seemed to have found a new lease on life at the local riding stables. But as she got older she became increasingly self-conscious, imagined other people were staring at her, pointing at her, and she started to hide by staying indoors. She stopped going to school and was allowed to have a home tutor. For the past year, she had become more or less a recluse, hardly speaking to anyone, shutting herself in her room for hours on end, her walls plastered with posters and pictures of horses and ponies. Holly had seen her, sometimes, talking with the horses that shared a field down the road. Claire would walk there in the evenings when it was quiet, her hood pulled up around her head, no matter how warm the weather. And she had watched her sister, blowing into their nostrils, communicating in a way she never did with even her own family.

Holly had suggested to their Dad that they buy her a pony, but he'd look exasperated and say, "How can we afford that? I'm working two jobs as it is." She felt sorry for him, and guilty once more. It was hard for him to cope with two young girls on his own. He worked all week as a truck driver and then weekends at a local garden center, just to make ends meet. So Holly had decided that she would save up and buy a pony for her sister. That was why she was working in the bookstore for the summer. She didn't want the money for herself. She wasn't interested in clothes or music or any of the things most of her school friends did. She just wanted her sister to be happy again. And the pony would be so much more than that – he would be Claire's friend, companion, protector, so he would have to be very special. Really steady, trustworthy, maybe an ex-police horse. She had thought it all out. Planned it. But she hadn't said a word to anyone. It would take her the whole summer to earn enough to add to her existing savings but she would do it. She had to. She owed it to Claire.

Even now, whenever she thought about what had happened, tears stung her eyes. She had been ten then and

Claire just six years old. Their mom hadn't been feeling well and had to go upstairs to lie down. She had asked Holly to keep an eye on Claire, who was wandering around the kitchen, bored, looking for things to do. At first, Holly tried to amuse her little sister, but then her favorite TV program came on.

"Come and watch, sis," she had said, but Claire didn't want to.

So Holly had plunked herself on the sofa, engrossed in the program she liked so much. She would never forget the bone-chilling scream that tore through the air just minutes later. She rushed into the kitchen, and Claire was on the floor, steam rising from her face, the kettle was beside her, with boiling water pouring onto the floor.

Afterwards, they had discovered that she had climbed onto a chair to get the kettle and switched it on, as she had seen their mother do countless times. She was trying to make a cup of tea for their mom, to make her better.

Holly never forgot the look of hate on her mother's face as they waited outside the hospital room. When her father arrived there, he hugged her mother, and they tried to comfort each other, excluding Holly completely. She had failed them and had let everyone down. They would never forgive her and she would never forgive herself.

She lost count of the operations Claire endured over

the years. Skin grafts, chronic pain, medication. Yet Claire never blamed her, not like their parents. And somehow that made it even worse.

The strain of the accident and its consequences took a toll on her parents' relationship. Maybe it had already been shaky, Holly sometimes wondered. She knew her mother felt terribly guilty that she had not been there for Claire. Her mother had left them and rarely visited them, and only occasionally called to see how they were. She never spoke to Holly again.

Nursing his grief, their father concentrated all his energies on Claire, showing her affection that never was there for Holly. Her sister's face was badly disfigured, maybe for life, despite all the work the plastic surgeons had undertaken. And it was all because of her own selfishness, Holly knew. She had ruined her sister's life and her father's too. She had lost her mother, and maybe her father's love. Sometimes it was too much to bear. But she had no choice. She had to deal with it.

The train was pulling away from the last stop now before she would arrive at her station. It gathered speed and then, unaccountably, slowed down and stopped. Signal failure, she wondered, or another train coming. She gazed at the urban scenery, the buildings, the shops, a block of apartments. Then she saw it. At first, she thought she must be seeing things. But there it was, standing as if it was the most natural thing in the world. A horse. Standing on the balcony of a high-rise block of apartments. Not just any horse, either. A golden horse.

Then the train jerked back to life and moved on, as the horse flashed past and was gone.

Chapter 3

"You were thrown clear. You were lucky." Her mom's words echoed in Jenni's ears as she lay in the hospital bed. Lucky? She wanted to spit the word back but she couldn't speak. Smokey was dead. How could she be lucky? It was a word she heard a lot over the next few days.

"You were lucky to escape with nothing more than cuts and bruises, and a mild concussion," several of the nurses pointed out to her. Her right leg was badly cut and painful, but she couldn't feel it. She couldn't feel anything. She didn't want them fussing over her. She just wanted to be left alone. But every time she closed her eyes, all she could see was Smokey, lying in the road, dying. She wanted to die, too.

She kept replaying the events in her mind, over and over. How could she have stopped it from happening? If only Ella had gotten her act together, gotten up on time for once, they would have ridden out together, taken a different route because Ella wanted to try out jumps across farmland. So Ella was partly to blame, and when she visited Jenni in hospital, Jenni wouldn't even look at her. And what about Jenni's mom, tempting fate by saying she loved Smokey too much. What a thing to say! It was easier to blame other people. But most of all Jenni blamed herself, and that was the hardest thing to bear. She recalled how Smokey had been reluctant to take the narrow road, as if he sensed something would happen. But she had made him anyway. She felt like she had let him down, because she had promised to protect him. She had rescued him, only for him to die on the road in agony. The guilt was too much for her.

When they said she could go home, she felt a mixture of relief that she could get away from the unwanted fuss of the nurses, but dread at how she would cope with being back without Smokey.

Her parents did their best, tried to be kind and

considerate, but it was hard to adjust to the change in their daughter.

"She'll get over it. Give her time," she heard her mom say to her Dad when they thought she was out of earshot. There were only two weeks of school to go, so they let her stay at home. Normally, Jenni would have looked forward to summer vacation – now she dreaded it. Everything seemed empty and meaningless.

"Maybe we can all go away somewhere warm, with nice beaches," suggested her Dad over supper one night. "A family vacation. We can ask Az to join us. He'll be on army leave again soon. What do you think, honey?"

But Jenni just stared blankly into space, like a robot. They hadn't been on a family vacation since she got Smokey, because she would never have wanted to leave him behind, not even for a week.

She couldn't sleep properly, because she had the same nightmare, again and again, which woke her screaming and distraught. She wouldn't open the curtains in her bedroom, because she couldn't bear to see the field where Smokey should have been.

She later learned that the two guys responsible for what had happened both came from her school. The one driving the car had been in the same hospital as she had, but no one told her till afterwards. Had she known, she would have wanted to hurt him like he'd hurt her.

He'd had both legs broken, a shattered collarbone, and a damaged spleen. *Good*, she'd said, to her mother's shock. *It should have been worse.*

One afternoon Ella turned up after school. Jenni was in the family room, apparently watching TV but not really taking it in. She heard her mom say to Ella in the kitchen, "I don't know what to do, Ella. I know she has to grieve, but I'm not sure she really accepts what's happened. She won't see a counselor and I'm worried sick."

"She must be devastated. Smokey meant the world to her," Ella replied sadly. "I never saw a pony and girl so attached to each other."

"Maybe we should get her another pony."

Ella shook her head. "Much too soon. It's only been a few weeks."

"She won't leave the house, Ella. I'm at my wits' end."

"I'll go and talk to her," Ella said gently.

Jenni stared coldly at her. "I'm not deaf, you know," she said.

"Your mom's really worried about you." Ella answered.

"No need. I'm fine."

"No you're not. Look, maybe if you had a ride on Dylan –"

"Is that supposed to make me feel better? Why should I want to ride another pony when Smokey is dead? I'll never ride again."

"Oh, Jenni," and Ella reached out her arms, wanting to give her friend a big hug, but Jenni backed away. "I just want to be left alone."

"If you change your mind…"

"I won't. Please go away."

With a hurt expression, Ella turned and left.

"There was no need for that," Jenni's mother pointed out, exasperated. "Ella is your friend. She was trying to help."

"Well, she shouldn't have bothered."

"Jenni, honey, please make an effort. You can't go on like this. You're making yourself ill. And me," she added.

For a moment, Jenni felt a twinge of guilt. She knew her mother cared about her and wanted to make it all better. Maybe she should try to face up to her fears. She shot a glance across the road, at Ella heading for the field.

"Okay," she said quietly.

Taking a deep breath, she got up, walked past her mother to the kitchen door and stepped outside. It felt strange to be standing at the gate, feeling the warmth of the sun. For a moment she watched Ella, chasing around the field after Dylan, as usual, and she actually smiled to herself. It was like old times, as if nothing had happened.

She imagined that Smokey was still there, and she could almost see him trotting up to the fence to greet her, brushing her hand with his whiskers. But he wasn't there. He wasn't there. And he never would be. Suddenly she felt sick. Turning quickly, she ran back into the house, up the stairs to her room, and buried her head in her pillow, sobbing her heart out.

On the morning of Jenni's birthday, her mother decided drastic action was needed.

"I think retail therapy is in order," she announced. "It works for me, so maybe it will work for you."

Jenni shrugged. "I don't care about clothes."

"All girls like clothes," her mom insisted. "Anyway, you need a change of scenery, you need to get away from here. Even for a few hours. So we're going into town."

"Not in the car?" Jenni had developed an unnatural hatred of cars since Smokey's death, to her mother's dismay.

"No. On the train. We can walk to the station from here; it's only ten minutes. Can you handle that?"

Jenni nodded. She had been trying harder lately. But it was difficult when she still felt so disconnected from the rest of the world around her.

It was a short and pleasant train journey, and Jenni found it surprisingly peaceful, gazing out of the window, listening to the train's rhythmic beat. Most of the passengers were school kids, and she hoped she wouldn't see anyone she knew. She didn't feel like engaging in conversation with anyone. Ella had brought over the schoolwork she had missed, so she could catch up over the summer vacation, but Jenni had little interest in history or geography right now.

Seeing that her daughter wasn't planning to chat, Jenni's mother turned on her iPod and listened to jazz music until the train arrived at the station.

They went into every clothes store in town, or so it seemed to Jenni, with her mom enthusiastically picking out dresses and tops that she thought her daughter might like. But her efforts were met with half-hearted interest, so eventually she gave up and started to look for things she would like for herself instead, while Jenni looked around the bookstore.

By the time they set off for home, Jenni had bought herself a couple of novels with the money her mom gave her for her birthday – more to please her than anything else – and her mom had two bags of stuff, mostly clothes.

"I feel awful about this," she said, as they squashed into the two remaining seats in the now busy train. It was after five, so they were riding with the commuters.

"No need," replied Jenni. "You like clothes. No reason why you shouldn't have some fun."

"At least you got your books," her mom replied, trying to make herself feel better.

There were people standing over them with hot, sweaty armpits, and the sun was blazing through the train windows. Jenni was relieved she didn't have to go to work every day on a stuffy train. Yet. Glancing around the train car, she saw a young mom with an irritable red-faced toddler. The mom was trying to keep him amused so he didn't scream and annoy the other passengers. Two men with briefcases were trying to read their newspapers and block out the rest of the world and a group of giggling teenage girls were gossiping and playing with their cell phones. And gazing out of the window was a girl who looked around the same age as Jenni, with dark, sad eyes and long black hair with alternating crimson and magenta streaks. She was dressed in black and Jenni wondered if she was in mourning, too. There was something distinctive about her, familiar even. Then Jenni realized she had seen her in the bookstore earlier, serving drinks in the coffee bar. She was still gazing intently out of the window when Jenni and her mom got off at their stop, oblivious to anything else.

"So, did you have a nice day, girls?" asked Jenni's Dad when they got back.

"Yes thanks," said Jenni dutifully.

"Jenni bought some books," said her mom.

"I don't need to ask what you bought," her Dad frowned, and Jenni's mom smiled sheepishly.

"I put it on the credit card," she said, hurrying upstairs with her purchases.

"No doubt," muttered Jenni's Dad, sighing. "By the way, Ella stopped by earlier. I told her to come back later. She said you can ride Dylan whenever you want, you know."

"But I don't want to."

"I think she misses you, Jen. I thought you were best friends."

"Smokey was my best friend."

Ella reappeared later that evening. "Happy birthday, Jenni. I bought you a present."

"Thanks."

"You can open it."

"Yes. I will." Awkwardly, Jenni unwrapped the gift Ella seemed so excited to give her. She felt a lump in her throat when she saw it was a small framed photograph of herself and Ella together, smiling and laughing, proudly holding up the rosettes they had won at the County Show. It was taken over a year ago, when everything had been normal and happy.

"Do you like it?" asked Ella nervously.

"Too many memories," said Jenni in a choked voice.

"We're drifting apart, Jenni. I don't want to lose you," said Ella desperately.

"I'm sorry. But seeing you and Dylan in the field across the road, where… it's like a constant reminder. I've tried to get over it, but I can't, not yet."

"What are you saying – that you don't want to be my friend any more?"

"I don't know."

"You have to try and deal with it, Jenni," Ella said, her upset turning to anger. "Because I can't do this much longer." She stormed out, leaving Jenni feeling worse than ever.

"Jenni, for goodness sake, she's trying her best to make you happy," said her mom. "But you won't give her a chance. She's about to give up. Do you really want to lose her friendship?"

"I resent her, Mom. I hate it, but I do."

"Because she still has Dylan?"

Jenni nodded. "I hate myself for feeling like this. It isn't fair, I know that."

"I understand it must be hard for you to see Ella's pony in that field every day, when Smokey is gone. But maybe you could overcome it if he wasn't the only pony there."

"What do you mean?"

"Your Dad and I, we thought about getting you another pony for your birthday –"

"I don't want another pony. Smokey can't be replaced."

"We're not saying another pony would replace him, but it would give you a focus, help you get over things, get back to normal again."

"I don't want another pony. Ever."

Jenni put the photo from Ella in the bottom of her dresser, along with all the photos of Smokey she had taken down off the bedside table and the walls, because it hurt too much to look at them. She went over to the window and looked out across the field. She wondered if the pain would ever go away.

By the next afternoon, however, Jenni wondered if it was too late to try and patch things up with Ella. She didn't really want to lose their friendship. They had shared so many good times together. So, seeing that Ella was in the field with Dylan, Jenni decided to go over and apologize.

The sky was overcast and Jenni wondered if a storm was brewing. It was difficult, crossing the road and leaning on the gate where Smokey would have waited for her. She tried to block the image out. Ella looked up in amazement when she saw Jenni, but she smiled.

"I just wanted to…" began Jenni awkwardly.

"Why don't you have a ride on Dylan? It'll only take me a minute to tack him up. Or you can help me."

"All right."

It felt strange, being so close to a pony again. Dylan fidgeted while Ella struggled with the girth, so Jenni held his head collar and rubbed his nose and ears, the way Smokey used to love. She felt a lump in her throat, and she forced herself to concentrate on keeping Dylan's head still.

"Thanks." Ella smiled appreciatively and Jenni thought for a moment that everything would be alright between them again after all. Maybe it wasn't as hard as she thought.

"Why don't you have a ride on Dylan? I would really like it if you did," said Ella.

Jenni considered this as she continued to stroke Dylan's silky ears. Maybe Ella and her parents were right, that she should just try to get back to normal, to do the things she used to love.

"Maybe…"

"Great. Do you need a leg up?"

"I'm fine thanks, I can manage," Jenni replied, though part of her wondered what she was doing. Ella was so eager to hand over her pony and it occurred to Jenni that Ella might have been feeling guilty about what had happened and needed to find a way to make up for things. Of course, she never could.

35

"Okay?"

Jenni nodded. But her mixed emotions were transmitting to Dylan and he tossed his head and fidgeted, uncertain of his new rider. Jenni walked him around a few times, and then trotted while Ella watched intently, anxiously.

"Feel okay?"

"I think so."

But Jenni felt like she was in a dream, fighting off memories of the last time she rode Smokey on that fateful day. She squeezed Dylan's sides and he glided effortlessly into a canter, smoother than any transition he had ever achieved with Ella, who felt a strange twinge of jealousy when she saw this. She always knew that Jenni was a better rider than she. But seeing her now, executing moves on her own pony that she knew he would not perform for her was difficult for Ella.

As Ella struggled with her mixed emotions, her hurt mingled with relief and joy that her friend was riding again, and that she had made it happen. Jenni started to enjoy her dream, the sensations of the movements of the horse beneath her, and without her even realizing it, Dylan was galloping. She felt adrenaline pump through her veins and for a moment it was wonderful. The wind was stinging her face and her eyes began to fill with water. She wasn't sure if it was just the wind or whether they were tears of joy or pain. Then images of Smokey began to flood her mind, and she saw him lying on the road, his final breath ebbing away, and she was consumed with guilt and an overwhelming sense of disloyalty. She couldn't see any more, on any level. She asked for halt and gradually Dylan slowed to a canter, trot, and walk. Again, his transitions were smooth and natural.

"What's wrong?" asked Ella. "You looked great out there."

"I can't do this. Not now, not ever," replied Jenni, sliding from the saddle. Her legs felt like jelly, or she would have simply run away as fast as she could.

"Jenni, talk to me please! What happened?"

But Jenni couldn't speak. She was too choked up with emotion.

"Jenni." Ella was shouting now. "Don't turn your back on me. I'm trying to help you!"

Being in the field, where Smokey should have been, felt so wrong. Everything felt wrong, and empty and hollow without Smokey.

"Jenni, come back! We have to talk. Don't walk out on me." The words sounded more distant now as Jenni climbed over the fence and set off in the opposite direction. She wanted to be anywhere else. She didn't care where.

"Jenni! If you go now, that's it. The end of our friendship!"

It was barely a whisper to Jenni. As the first drops of rain fell, she felt her legs return to normal and she started to run. She didn't look back.

She didn't know how long she was running, only that the rain was pouring down now, and her T-shirt was soaked through. But she kept on running – she didn't want to stop. She didn't know what she was running from, but just knew she had to get away from Ella, Dylan, her parents, and the memories that hurt so much. When she was finally out of breath, she realized she was in the woods where she had ridden so many times with Smokey. It was one of their favorite places, but it looked different today somehow, with the light fading and the sky dark from the storm. For the first time ever, the woods suddenly seemed threatening. The ground was slippery and her boots skidded in the mud. She stopped for a moment, trying to get her bearings. Could she be lost? How could that be possible, when she had been here so many times before? But it all looked unfamiliar for some reason. She hurried on, her eyes so blinded by tears that she didn't notice the huge hole only steps away, where a tree had been uprooted. The sound of a pony whinnying in alarm made her stop in her tracks at the last minute.

She spun around.

"Ella?"

So Ella and Dylan must have come after her, but as

she peered through the trees, she could see no sign of them. Stepping forward, she saw the huge pit beneath her and realized that if she hadn't been distracted by the whinny, she would have been in big trouble. She was shivering now with her wet clothes plastered to her skin.

"Thanks Ella," she called out, expecting any minute to see Ella and Dylan up ahead. But all that greeted her was cold silence. And delayed shock.

It hit her now that she had been inches away from the deep water-filled hole. One more step and she would have fallen in, possibly even drowned. And no one would have known where she was. She was trembling now. She should call home. They would be worried about her. Fumbling with her cell phone, she held it up to the dim light. No signal. Useless.

"Well, Jenni you really have done it this time, you idiot," she said to herself as reality hit. "You wanted to be alone and now you really are."

Then, as she looked ahead, trying to decide which direction to set off in, she saw it, by a nearby oak tree. The outline of a pony, watching her. A gray pony. So very familiar.

"Smokey?"

She stared, transfixed. Was she going insane? She closed her eyes tightly, held her breath and counted to ten. When she opened them again, she was sure the pony would be gone. But there he was. Waiting for her.

"Smokey." She was certain now. But how could that be possible?

Then the pony moved away, knowing she would follow. Very soon, Jenni found herself coming to an opening in the woods, and a path she recognized. She could find her way home now. She glanced down at her cell phone. The signal was back. But when she looked up again the pony was gone.

"Smokey. Please come back." But deep down she knew she was alone again.

Jenni was puzzled. Had she imagined it? Or had Smokey's ghost really come back to warn her of danger and guide her safely out of the woods, keeping the unspoken promise they had made to protect each other? Whatever had happened, the pony had saved her life.

Desperately she called for him, but the only sounds to come back were the empty echoes of her frantic cries in the lonely woods.

Chapter 4

Holly just couldn't get the horse on the balcony out of her head. She wanted to tell someone, but there was no one to tell. She didn't really have any friends now and she didn't feel she deserved any. After the accident, people seemed to shun her – at least that's how it felt. And how could she blame them? She had always been a bit of a loner, but Jacquie, who she thought was her best friend at the time, stopped hanging out with her. It happened gradually, not right away, which made it seem worse. When they had spoken about it, Jacquie admitted that she didn't like coming to the house any more. She said the atmosphere was so tense and awful, she felt embarrassed if she caught sight of Claire, and she didn't know how to deal with it. So they just drifted apart.

Holly missed having someone to talk to and confide in, but as time went on she got used to it and was content with her own thoughts and company. She threw herself into her schoolwork and got great exam results, not that her Dad seemed impressed, which saddened her. So she focused all her energies on that and looking after her sister. She never went out anywhere for fun. It just didn't feel right somehow.

Of course, she talked to Claire, who was her only friend, but for some reason she didn't feel she could mention the horse to her. Not yet anyway. She even wondered if she had imagined it. After all, a horse on a balcony wasn't exactly what you would expect to see from a train window.

So she resigned herself to another Saturday night at home preparing pizza, and salad for her Dad and sister, with strained conversation at the table. Then she would go to her room and read until she fell asleep, while Claire played on her computer. Her Dad would be working at the garden center on Sunday, so after breakfast she would probably go for a long walk if the weather was good, or take a ride on her ancient bike.

"The pizza is already in the oven. Cheese," Claire

said, meeting her at the gate. She seemed unusually cheerful.

"Thanks."

"Saves you having to do it when you've been at work all day. Dad's just getting a shower and I'm hungry. Are you?"

"A bit," replied Holly, pleased that her sister seemed so upbeat.

Later, when they were finishing their meal, Claire announced, "I've made a decision. I'm going to ride again."

A brief silence greeted her statement while Claire and her father looked at each other, surprised and pleased. But mostly very surprised.

"Well that sounds great," said their father a little hesitantly. "When did you decide this?"

"Oh, I've been thinking about it for awhile now. I miss being with horses."

"I know. And if I could afford to buy you a pony of your own, you know that I would."

"I know that, Dad. I know you would do anything for me." Claire replied.

Their Dad looked at his youngest daughter with a love in his face that seemed reserved exclusively for her. Holly saw it, and although she was familiar with it, she still felt a sharp pain of jealousy. She missed his affection.

"Where will you be riding?" she asked, wondering if

Claire had a new friend with a pony who was willing to share. But she doubted that. Claire never went out to see old friends or make new ones.

"The riding school. I used to really enjoy going there."

Before the accident, thought Holly. When the only looks she got from people were of admiration for her riding skills and her pretty face.

Her father had some reservations. "Are you sure about this?"

"Of course. I'm nervous," replied Claire. "Not about riding. But… you know."

"Yes. Remember, you don't have to do anything you don't want to do, sweet pea."

"But I should try, Dad. I can't spend the rest of my life living like this, can I? There's a world out there."

Her words were like music to Holly's ears. Words she never thought she would hear her sister ever utter. And for a second, she felt her burden of guilt begin to shift. If Claire was okay again, if she could lead a normal life again… Though it was hard to imagine any of them having a normal life again. Holly was devoted to her sister but she also felt trapped by her, and resentful and guilty for having those feelings.

"I think it's great. A terrific idea," she said. "When did you have in mind?"

"Tomorrow."

"Tomorrow?" Their Dad sounded worried again.

"I already called the riding school."

Wow. That's a change. Better and better, thought Holly.

"Three-ish seems to be a good time. And I checked and they still have Pippa."

Pippa was the pony Claire had ridden when she rode there regularly and she had formed a close bond with the sweet-natured mare.

"Will you come with me, Holly?"

Holly was taken aback. She hadn't expected this. Although she shared her sister's love of horses, she had no desire to ride them. They were too big and scary.

"I don't think so, Claire."

"Please. Pleeeeeease."

Her father shot Holly an accusatory glance, daring her to refuse her sister.

"Okay."

"Great. It'll be fun!"

Holly was shaking in her shoes at the very thought of getting on a horse, but it was great to see Claire smile again. As she got up to clear away the plates, Holly noticed how thoughtful their Dad looked. "I have to make a phone call," he said getting up.

When he returned he said, "Now it's my turn to make an announcement," and Holly wondered if this was destined to be a night of surprises.

"Guess what? I'm coming with you girls tomorrow. I managed to get some time off at the garden center. They're letting me finish at 2 p.m. so I can join you both!"

"Awesome," yelled Claire, throwing her arms around her Dad's neck. "I'm so happy now!"

"Even better, I'm going to ride with you."

Holly was stunned. "But you don't know how to ride."

He grinned. "Well maybe I should learn then."

And for the first time in ages, there was laughter in the house. Suddenly, Holly saw a different future, a future she had never dared hope for. The family was all together and riding every Sunday. Sharing time and fun. They were a real unit again. She had the best night's sleep in years, and no nightmares.

The next morning, Claire got out her jodhpurs, which she hadn't worn for years.

"They still fit me!" she exclaimed in delight. She seemed so excited. They all were.

"Will this do?" asked their Dad, parading in worn jeans and a faded T-shirt.

"Just about," grinned Claire.

As they piled into the battered van that their Dad drove, Holly kept wondering if this was all a dream and that any minute now she would wake up. But half an hour later they were at the riding school, seeing the stables up close with horses and riders in the yard. Reality hit home and Holly felt butterflies in her stomach at just the thought of actually getting onto a horse.

"Well, this is it. The moment of truth," said their Dad as they were led over to the stable block. Claire wondered if he felt nervous too.

Kerry, their instructor, said, "We have two lovely, quiet horses who are good for beginners. So Holly, I've teamed you with Cobra, who's very gentle, and your Dad will be on Kickstart, the skewbald cob."

Holly regarded the big gray gelding, Cobra, with a degree of suspicion. "He's huge," she said anxiously. "I'll need a stepladder just to get on him."

Kerry laughed. "You can use the mounting block, and I'll help you with a leg up."

She turned to Claire. "I know you won't need any help getting on, will you? I remember you were a very competent rider."

But Claire wasn't listening. "Where's Pippa?"

"Sorry, but she went lame so we thought you might like to try Prelude instead. She's very steady and calm, but she'll give you a nice ride." She unhooked the reins of a dark gray mare and handed them to Claire, who didn't conceal her disappointment.

"Hey, you can ride Pippa next time," suggested Holly,

not wanting the day to be spoiled in any way. "Anyway, Prelude looks nice don't you think?"

But when Claire dropped the reins over Prelude's head, the horse put her ears back, as if she could sense something wasn't right.

"She's just a bit miffed she has to wait for her dinner," said Kerry briskly, hastily trying to smooth things over. Like Holly, she had noticed that two of the stable girls were staring at Claire. "Be firm with her."

"Maybe she doesn't like me," muttered Claire under her breath, but they pretended not to hear.

Soon they were all mounted, and Claire started to look more confident as they formed a little procession toward the riding ring. Holly felt as if she were ten feet off the ground, and her legs were like jelly. She longed to have both feet safely on the ground again, but she wanted to do this for her sister and Dad. If she could get used to riding, maybe it could become a regular thing for all three of them. Together. There was a lot at stake on this ride.

The sun was shining, Claire looked happy on Prelude and their Dad was smiling as he struggled to keep upright on Kickstart.

"We'll just do some walking and trotting today," said Kerry. "Nothing too ambitious, so it will be nice and relaxed."

Holly didn't think she would ever get used to how strange it felt be in the saddle but Claire looked very much at home. After awhile, when Kerry was convinced that her two new beginners understood how to steer and stop their mounts, she decided it was time to trot.

"You can hold on to the pommel if you don't feel secure," she advised Holly.

"What's the pommel?"

"The front of the saddle," said Claire, pleased that she remembered such things.

"You go first, Dad," suggested Holly, terrified that she would fall off.

"Promise not to laugh," he replied.

"Can't promise that," giggled Claire.

"Shorten the reins and give a little squeeze with your legs to push your horse into a trot," said Kerry.

Finally, after a good deal of persuasion, Kickstart lumbered into an awkward trot and their Dad bounced up and down in an undignified fashion.

"Like a sack of potatoes," teased Claire.

"I heard that," retorted their Dad but he was grinning, enjoying the joke at his expense. "This hurts!"

"Your turn next, Holly."

This is fun, thought Holly as she nervously pushed Cobra into a brisk trot. Too brisk, she thought, as he snatched at the reins, and she felt her weight tipping off balance. Struggling to stay on, she gripped the pommel until Cobra came to an abrupt halt.

"Well done," said Kerry.

"Now let's see Claire and Prelude show us how it's done," said their Dad.

Claire sat up straight in the saddle, shoulders back, looking every inch the experienced rider. But Holly sensed something was not quite right, and that her sister was anxious. As she set off down the ring, Prelude spooked for no apparent reason, and proceeded to do a half trot, half canter, while Claire struggled to regain control.

"She doesn't like me. She's scared of me!" Claire yelled.

But Kerry was not accepting that. "Nonsense, Claire. She probably just heard a noise that we didn't notice. You know how sensitive horses can be."

Claire wasn't convinced. "She hates me. I wish I was riding Pippa."

"Don't be like that. Horses don't have emotions like us," ventured their Dad. "Let's face it, they're not very bright creatures."

It was the wrong thing to say. Both Kerry and Claire glared at him.

"Oops," muttered Holly under her breath. At this rate their perfect day would begin to fall apart. Maybe it already had.

"Let's all try that again," said Kerry when Claire trotted back to the gate.

This time their Dad had improved his technique and managed to take better control of Kickstart, executing a surprisingly smooth trot.

"Excellent," remarked Kerry. "We'll make a rider out of you yet!"

He looked pleased with himself. "I'm enjoying this," he admitted, "more than I thought I would."

"That was good, Dad," said Holly, wishing she didn't have to go again. But after some encouragement from Kerry, Cobra launched into a vaguely rhythmic trot and Holly succeeded in getting around the ring without falling off. She took a sneaky glance at her watch, hoping the lesson was almost over.

But Claire was clearly having problems with Prelude, who danced and shied, the horse's ears pinned back on her head.

"I don't know what's gotten into her today," said Kerry. "She isn't usually like this."

"I told you, it's me. She doesn't like me."

"No way. Just keep her head up, and squeeze with your legs. That's it."

But the words had hardly left her mouth when Prelude suddenly circled rapidly before bolting off toward the stable, with Claire unable to stop her.

51

"Oh no, she isn't going to stop," said Dad, his voice panicky. "She's going to crash into the gate!"

"Or jump over it," added Holly, her face white.

They watched helplessly as Prelude took off over the five-barred gate, rapping it with her forelegs and landing badly, sending Claire flying over the horse's head.

Their Dad jumped off Kickstart and was running over to his daughter, while Holly struggled to dismount. By the time she reached her sister, a crowd had gathered.

"She's badly hurt," said one person, "Look at the poor girl's face."

"Call an ambulance," said another.

"Are you okay honey?" asked their Dad. "Are you hurt?"

"No, but these people keep staring at me," she said, trying to cover her face with her hands, clearly overwhelmed. "Tell them to go away."

"They're trying to help. They want to make sure you're okay," he said.

"They just want to laugh at me," said Claire, rolling into a ball and sobbing.

"Of course they don't," said Holly, trying to comfort her sister, who was rapidly withdrawing, as she had done before.

"Is she hurt?" asked Kerry, full of concern.

"She says she's alright. I'll get her into the van," said their Dad, scooping his daughter up into his arms. The lively girl of an hour before had turned into a limp rag doll that just wanted to hide from the world.

"Sure you're okay, baby? Did you hurt your head? Did that horse trample you?"

"I'm fine. I was thrown clear," she replied. "I just want to be on my own. Don't want people looking at me and pitying me."

"No one's doing that sis," said Holly, trying to give Claire a hug. But she was pushed away.

"Don't touch me. No one touch me. It was a mistake to come out. I should have known. I want to go home."

They drove home in silence.

"I'll make some iced tea," said Holly, but no one responded.

Then the phone rang. Sighing, their Dad answered. After a short conversation he hung up, saying, "The Garden Center had problems with some vandals today. They smashed some greenhouses and the place is a mess. They need some help to clean up. Perfect end to a perfect day," he growled. "I'll be as fast as I can. Holly, make sure you look after your sister."

He drove away.

"Would you like a drink or something to eat?"

Claire just looked right past her and said, "I should wear a mask. Will you make me a mask?" Then she ran upstairs to her room and slammed the door.

Numb, Holly was still sitting in the kitchen staring into space when her Dad returned.

"Is your sister alright?" he asked.

"She shut herself in her room and hasn't been out," Holly replied.

"I'll go and see how she is," and he disappeared up the stairs. Minutes later he came down. "Are you sure she was in her room?"

"Yes, of course. What's wrong?"

"She's not there. Or anywhere else upstairs!"

"She must be. I would have heard her come down."

"Maybe you fell asleep or just didn't notice." There was an edge to his voice that made her feel sick. "I asked you to look after her Holly!"

"She must be in the house!"

But when they had both finished searching the house, Holly's sense of unease was escalating rapidly.

"She isn't here," said her Dad. "Where is my daughter?"

Chapter 5

"Maybe we should consider taking her to see a psychiatrist," said Jenni's mother in despair. "I really don't know what else to do."

"All that stuff about seeing a ghost in the woods. She was in a terrible state when she got back the other night. I was worried sick!"

Jenni was crouched on the landing listening and reflecting on what had happened. She wasn't surprised her parents didn't believe her when she told them she'd seen Smokey's ghost, but she hadn't quite been prepared for how badly they had taken it.

Even Ella thought she was going nuts. But she knew what she had seen; she knew that Smokey had saved her. It didn't matter what they thought. What mattered was seeing Smokey again.

It was Ella who had found her on the edge of the woods. When Jenni had run off, Ella's initial reaction was one of anger. She felt she had tried everything to mend their friendship, but that Jenni was just throwing it back in her face.

When she had calmed down, and realized Jenni had set off in the rain as if it wasn't there, she became concerned and decided to go after her on Dylan. When there was no sign of her in their usual haunts, Ella started to panic. What if something bad happened to Jenni after their argument? She would have *even more* to feel guilty about. How could she face Jenni's parents? Her mind was working overtime, trying to filter out awful scenarios. And to make matters worse, Dylan made his feelings known about his dislike of being out in the rain, shying at every opportunity. It was ironic that he had been so well behaved with Jenni – she resented it, but felt guilty about having such feelings.

How many times she wished she could turn the clock back. She would have given anything to have everything back to normal, with her and Jenni best friends again. Riding out together with Dylan and Smokey, chatting about life, the universe and lots in between. She tried to call Jenni on her cell phone, but there was no signal. She wondered if it was because of the rain, or the fact that she was approaching the woods, which was in a valley. Dylan gave a little snort, as if to say, "No way," when she steered him toward the woodland path she and Jenni had often used on their rides.

"You're probably right, boy," she admitted. "It would be crazy to ride in there today. With the rain, it'll be slippery and muddy, far too treacherous for a pony." And a human, she thought, hoping that Jenni had not chosen this path.

They sheltered under a big oak tree for awhile until Ella decided what the best course of action was. She concluded that she would turn for home and face Jenni's parents. As she prepared to ride away, Dylan suddenly pricked his ears up and seemed more alert, as if he was listening to something. At this point he would have normally pulled the reins from her hands to get back to his warm stable, so she looked around frantically for signs of whatever had distracted him. The rain continued to drum down but through it she could make out a muffled sound. Like someone sobbing.

"Jenni? Is that you?"

There was no reply, but she figured out where it was coming from and urged Dylan to walk in the direction of the sound. Then she saw Jenni. Huddled on the grass, crying.

At first, Jenni didn't seem to notice Ella, even when she was next to her and asked, "Jen, are you okay? What happened?" When Jenni's tear-stained face met hers, Ella wondered if her friend was hysterical, because what she was saying didn't make any sense.

"I saw Smokey. He saved me and I saw him. He was here!"

"But that's not possible, Jen, you know that. Did something happen in the woods? Did you get lost?"

"Lost. He led me out. Saved my life! I could have drowned."

Ella decided not to push at first, being more concerned about getting Jenni safely back to her probably frantic parents. "Come on, get up behind me on Dylan and I'll take you home. You must be frozen."

Jenni gave her a blank look, as if she was disconnected from the real world, Ella thought. She reached out her hand. Jenni still held back and the two girls stared at each other, their eyes meeting, acknowledging the conflict that was going on for each of them and somehow trying to make sense of it all. Then Jenni took Ella's outstretched hand and climbed up behind her. They rode home in silence.

The next day, however, when Ella went to see if Jenni was feeling any better, the atmosphere between them quickly became strained and frosty.

"There are no such things as ghosts," Ella told her impatiently. "I know you want to see Smokey again, but that doesn't mean he was there. You wanted it so badly, you made yourself believe it."

"But he saved my life," Jenni persisted.

"You're not listening to me, are you? Listen, Jenni, I really think you've lost it this time. You have to get over this. Smokey's gone. I know it's hard, but –"

"You have no idea what it's like," Jenni snapped.

Ella stared at her friend coldly. She was angry, hurt, and exasperated. She opened her mouth to reply and then turned and walked away. Jenni knew this time she had lost her friend for good. She was truly alone.

Realizing she had to somehow appease her parents if she was to escape the unwelcome interference of a psychiatrist, Jenni pretended she had imagined the ghost and that she would try really hard to get back to normal. She did a convincing job and her relieved parents eventually, and willingly, accepted this. In the meantime, Jenni took walks out in the woods, spending hours just sitting, hoping to see Smokey's ghost once more. But nothing happened.

And then there was Ella. She saw Ella most days, in the field or riding on Dylan. She did her best to avoid Ella, staying in the house when she was around. She did not want to speak to her. There was nothing to say. Besides, she still harbored resentment at the situation, a painful reminder of what she was missing now that Smokey was gone.

The strain of trying to make her parents believe she was coping, when inside she felt only despair, began to take its toll. Finally she came to a very disturbing conclusion. Smokey had come to her aid when she was in danger. So she decided the only way she would get to see Smokey again was to put herself in danger once more. Slowly, Jenni began to formulate a plan.

Chapter 6

Holly wondered if her father would ever forgive her. If anything happened to Claire… again… she just couldn't bear to think about it.

"Where could she have gone?" he demanded almost accusingly.

"I don't know."

"Did she take her cell phone?"

"I don't know."

"I'll call it." He dialed, punching the numbers into the

61

phone furiously. Then he slammed it down. "Turned off. Wherever her phone is, it's turned off."

She doesn't want to be found, thought Holly, feeling more worried than ever.

"We've searched the house, and she's not here." He sounded desperate. "Maybe we missed something. We'd better search again."

Holly looked in Claire's bedroom for clues. Anything that might help. Maybe she kept a diary. She scoured the surface of the dressing table, checked the drawers but found nothing.

This can't be happening, she thought. She stood at the bedroom window and stared hopelessly. The light was only just starting to fade but Holly already felt engulfed in darkness.

"Maybe she went to the stables," suggested Holly.

"Call and find out," Her father replied.

But the stable had not seen Claire since the fateful lesson earlier. They did agree to search just in case.

"What about her friends?"

"She doesn't really have any. Just me."

Her father looked at her. Holly felt she could almost hear the words that must have been in his mind – *And what a great friend you are*. But he didn't say them. Instead he announced, "I'm going out to the woods to search."

"I'll come with you," she offered.

"No, I want you to stay here in case she comes back. I don't want her coming back to an empty house."

"But I want to help," Holly retorted.

"Stay here." It was an order this time. He grabbed a large heavy-duty flashlight and slammed the door.

Waiting alone was agony. Holly kept trying Claire's cell phone, just in case. She sent text messages begging her sister to call, hoping that any moment their father would be back, with Claire safe. She paced the house, unable to settle down.

Midnight came and went but there was no sign of her father or sister. Holly felt exhausted but her brain was awake, working overtime, and she wondered if she would ever sleep again. Finally, at two in the morning, her father returned and she dared to hope.

"I can't find her," he said wearily. He sounded defeated.

Holly wondered what to say but there were no words left.

"I'm calling the police," he said.

It was the worst night Holly could remember in a long time. She lay awake till around 4 a.m., and then drifted into uneasy slumber. At 5 a.m. she heard her father moving in the kitchen, probably making coffee. She wondered if he had slept at all.

Then at 6:30 a.m. she was awoken again by the sound of the toilet flushing. Fed up with tossing and turning, she got up and decided to make herself and her father a hot drink. Passing the open door of Claire's bedroom, she was alarmed and surprised to see a shape in the bed, curled up under the comforter. Full of trepidation she crept in, making her way slowly toward the bed.

"Claire?" she laid her hand gently on the reclining figure, which moved suddenly.

"Holly, you made me jump. I was trying to sleep!"

"Sleep? Claire, are you all right? What happened?" asked Holly.

"Nothing happened. I just needed to be on my own for awhile. But I'm home now, so there's nothing to worry about." She pulled the comforter up over her head and closed her eyes.

Holly was dumbfounded. Relieved. Amazed. Angry. Her sister was safe. She felt like shaking her, demanding to know where she had been. Didn't she realize they were all worried sick, that the police had been called? How selfish was she, not even telling them when she came home again? But instead, Holly calmly turned and tiptoed downstairs to find her father, still dressed, dozing on the sofa, clutching a photo of Claire as a baby. For a moment, Holly just studied him. She felt an overwhelming sadness. It was she who should have run away. Would he have been like this, clutching her picture, if she had gone missing? But no tears flowed; she had cried all the tears she had, a long time ago. She would let him sleep for awhile longer. Just until she had made them both a hot drink.

Jenni realized that the plan she had formulated was drastic to say the least. So before putting it into action, she went back to the woods once more, hoping she would find Smokey again. She kept retracing her steps the day he had appeared to her, managing to find the place she nearly died. She sat for hours, staring into space, replaying what had happened that day and each time she came to the same conclusion. Smokey had saved her from danger. Life threatening danger. He was her guardian angel and although she couldn't see him, he was still around, watching out for her, as they had promised each other. When she realized what she had to do, she felt a little frightened. After all, what if she got it wrong? She wrestled with the problem, trying to see if she could figure out another way. But there really was no other option. She brooded on it, unable to tell another soul, not that she now had a friend to talk to any more. Her parents would have thought she was crazy. Maybe she was. She even began to doubt herself. Until she had the dream.

She was standing on the edge of a cliff, peering down

a steep drop onto the rocks below. Someone, Az perhaps, was telling her to jump. But she was frozen to the spot, too scared to move. Then, suddenly, she lost her balance and was falling. The sensation of cutting through the air was both exhilarating and terrifying. But the next minute she was riding again – except she was still in the air – as if the horse she was riding had wings!

Now she knew for certain that he was waiting for her.

When Holly told her father that his daughter had returned, he ran upstairs and hugged Claire, crying with joy. After he left for work, Holly tried to quiz her sister about what happened.

"Where did you go, Claire? We looked everywhere for you."

"Why does it matter? I'm back now."

"You must have known we were worried sick. Especially Dad. How could you put him though that?"

"Sorry. I just had to get away," she replied.

And despite Holly's questions, Claire still refused to say where she had been.

"Well, I suppose all that matters is that you are home and safe. But you have to promise not to disappear like that again."

Claire shrugged. "I promise." But the words sounded hollow somehow and Holly was unconvinced. She would have to keep an extra special eye on her sister when she was home. For now, she had to go to work and pray that Claire would still be there when she got back.

As she set off down the road for the station, Holly felt a little reassured that their father was coming home at lunchtime to see Claire. She would not be alone all day at least. Claire needed friends, but it was another matter convincing her sister of that.

The sky was overcast with heavy rain forecasted for later. Holly hoped she would make it to the station before the downpour. As she approached the station, there was a small group of people gathered outside the entrance, their voices raised, and she wondered what was going on. Had something happened? Then she saw the sign, *Station Closed Today*.

"What's going on?" she asked a uniformed official.

"Closed, dear. Sorry."

"But why? What's going on?" she pressed further.

"Burst water main. Station flooded."

"But how will I get to work?" asked Holly.

"Trains will start from the next stop on the line. If you want to wait, we're trying to arrange for a special bus to the next station. But there might be a bit of a delay."

Holly considered this. The next station was a fifteen-minute walk and she would probably get there before the bus did.

"Okay. Thanks," she answered and she set off purposefully along the country roads as the clouds darkened and the rain began to fall. She was wondering if she would see the horse on the balcony today.

Full of resolve now about what had to be done, Jenni told her mom she wanted to go shopping again, but on her own this time.

"That's great! It's a really positive step!" Her mom answered. Her mom, for whom retail therapy worked wonderfully well when she was feeling low, was pleased, interpreting this as a sign that her daughter was indeed getting back to normal. Jenni had been increasingly withdrawn and both her parents were at their wits end, wondering if Jenni would ever be back to her normal self.

"How much money do you need?" Her mother asked her.

"Well, the train fare. Not much really. I'm not going to go crazy shopping." She reflected for a moment on her choice of words. If her mom, or indeed, anyone, knew what she was planning to do, they would indeed think she was crazy.

"What are you going to be buying? Clothes? CDs?"

"I don't know yet. I'm just going to have a look at the stores. I might pop into that bookstore." She was surprised at how easily she was able to lie.

"Well, have a great time. Take as long as you like."

She gave her daughter a hug, and for a moment Jenni felt scared. Then she told herself she had nothing to lose, not now.

She wanted to walk to the station, but it was raining and her mom insisted on giving her a lift in the car.

"I want to make sure you get there safe and sound," her mom said, and Jenni had to push another wave of guilt to the back of her mind. She had opted for a mid-morning train, thinking it wouldn't be too busy at the station, but when they arrived, the place was thronging with people.

"It isn't normally so busy at this time of day," remarked her mom. "I wonder if something's happened? I'd better go to the ticket office with you."

"No need, Mom, I'll be fine," replied Jenni anxiously, hoping her mom would not insist on waiting with her until the train arrived. That would mess up her plans.

Upon asking a policewoman if there was a problem, they were informed that the station just down the line had been temporarily closed due to a burst water main. So the train had been diverted, which meant the passengers from the other station had to board there. "I hope you get a seat on the train, honey. It's boring to have to stand. Do you want me to wait with you?"

"Thanks Mom, but I'll be fine and I really don't mind standing."

"Well alright, only if you're sure." She gave her daughter a kiss on the cheek. "Have a fun day, Jenni. See you later!"

The guilt was there again as Jenni watched her mom drive away.

She looked around at her fellow passengers to distract herself, but all she could think about was the train, due to arrive at any moment. She walked up and down the platform, counting the minutes. Soon. Soon it would be done. She took a deep breath.

Then came the garbled voice over the loudspeaker – the train was running late. Five minutes late. Why did it have to be late? She didn't need any complications. She began to count the seconds. Five times sixty. She had to time it right.

"Twenty one, twenty two, twenty three…"

She walked down the platform. She had to be in the right place at the right time.

"Forty five, forty six…" She could see the train now, making its way through the tunnel to the station platform.

Not long now. "Fifty three, fifty four…"

The train was close now, slowing down, but still fast enough for her purpose. If she was right, Smokey would save her again.

"Fifty six, fifty seven, fifty eight…"

She hesitated on the edge of the platform, her eyes scanning for a sign.

"Fifty nine, sixty." Closing her eyes, Jenni took a step forward. As her foot hovered in mid air she suddenly felt a jolt of fear. What if she was wrong? What if Smokey did not come? But she was already off balance, about to fall, and it was too late to save herself!

Chapter 7

Suddenly a pair of hands grabbed Jenni firmly by the
shoulders and pulled her sharply back, away from
the edge of the platform. Stunned, she turned to be
confronted by a pale girl with red-streaked black hair,
about her own age, who for some reason looked strangely
familiar.

Still shocked by what happened, Jenni tried to
push the girl away. Her feelings were in turmoil – the
relief of being safe was mixed with annoyance and

disappointment. Now she would never know if Smokey would have saved her.

"What do you think you're doing? You could have been killed," demanded Holly.

"Don't be ridiculous. I knew what I was doing and I wouldn't have come to any harm," said Jenni, knowing that this was probably a lie on both accounts.

Holly frowned. "Now that's a scary thing to say. Maybe you need some help."

"Leave me alone. I can do what I want and it's none of your business." Jenni replied.

"That's debatable."

The girl was looking at Jenni very strangely and she realized that what she had just said sounded bizarre, to say the least. She had to say something that would convince the girl to go away, make her think everything was normal.

"I wasn't trying to jump, if that's what you think." Holly told the girl matter-of-factly.

"You could have fooled me," retorted Holly. "I've been watching you. I know exactly what you were planning to do."

"Watching me? Why were you watching me? You must be crazy."

Holly laughed. "Oh, so throwing yourself in front of a train isn't crazy?"

"I wasn't going to," said Jenni.

"So you say."

"How long were you watching me?"

"Long enough."

"Why?"

"Something about you didn't feel right. You seemed… preoccupied. I just had this feeling…"

"Feelings usually get people into trouble."

"Well, I got you out of trouble."

"What makes you think that?" Jenni started to walk away. The platform was nearly empty now, the crowds having jostled each other to get onto the train in an attempt to get a seat. She didn't want to be left alone with this strange girl who was starting to freak her out.

"Hey, don't walk away. We haven't finished here yet!"

Jenni turned abruptly. "Stop following me. You'd better get on that train or you'll miss it. Don't you have somewhere else to go? That's why you're here, isn't it? Like everyone else doing their normal, everyday stuff."

Holly felt the pain in the girls words and saw it in her eyes.

"If you only knew how much I would like to be normal," Holly said bitterly. And this time Jenni felt her own pain being reflected back. For a split second, the two girls realized they shared a connection. Scared by it, Jenni walked away again. "I have to go," she said quickly.

74

"I'll come with you. You shouldn't be alone."

Jenni tried to ignore her, striding purposefully… to where? Then she stopped in her tracks. Where was she going? She hadn't thought beyond her plan. She should have been reunited with Smokey by now, riding bareback away from here, away from grief and sadness. Now she had to rethink everything. She wasn't ready to go home yet. She felt like she didn't belong anywhere. Maybe she should try again or think of another plan to bring Smokey back. She felt as if the world was crumbling around her. Then she felt a hand on her shoulder, but this time it was gentle, tentative even. And comforting.

"I think you need to talk," suggested Holly kindly.

Jenni tried to swallow the lump in her throat. "There's nothing to talk about."

But Holly persisted. "I think there is."

The next few minutes were a blur for Jenni, but before she knew it, she was sitting in the tiny deli at the station with the raven-haired girl who said her name was Holly.

"I'm Jenni. Thanks for the soda. Am I keeping you from something? I mean, you were waiting for the train so you must have been going somewhere."

"I feel like I'm going nowhere most of the time," joked Holly, adding, "I was on my way to work at the bookstore. Just for the summer."

"The big bookstore in town? With the café?" asked Jenni.

Holly nodded.

"I thought you looked familiar. I've seen you on the train!"

"So we've both been spying on each other," laughed Holly. "We both must be a little weird."

"My parents think I'm weird," said Jenni. "And my best friend. Well, ex-best friend."

"Why ex-best friend?"

"We had a falling out. Big time. I said some really awful things. She tried to put things right, but I suppose I just didn't care anymore." She took a sip of sweet, sticky soda. "I don't want you to get fired because of me."

"I won't. I'll call and let them know I'll be late," replied Holly, fishing a cell phone from her shoulder bag. When she had finished she said, "So why do people think you're weird?"

Jenni hesitated, wondering if she should censor what she felt like saying. But then again, she had nothing to lose really, since Holly had already seen her at her most extreme. And after today they would probably never meet again.

"Okay, well if you really want to know, I saw the ghost of my dead horse in the woods. And no one believes me. I mean, why would they, because ghosts don't exist, right?

Only he didn't *just* appear – he saved me from drowning. And I've been longing and praying and wishing that he would come back again, but he hasn't."

As Holly considered this statement, she realized why Jenni was about to step off the platform. "So you thought that if your life was in danger again, then your horse would save you?"

Jenni smiled sadly. "That's about the sum of it. So how do you feel about sharing a soda with a lunatic?"

"Well, your idea did have a certain logic, I'll admit that," replied Holly thoughtfully. "What was your horse called?"

"Smokey."

"Do you want to talk about him?"

"Yes and no. It hurts even thinking about him. He was my whole world. We had such a strong connection and I miss him so much."

"My sister, Claire, she loves horses," Holly told her new friend.

"Really? Does she ride?"

"She used to. Did recently, only it didn't really work out."

"Why not?" asked Jenni.

"Claire had an accident when she was little and it had a major effect on her, on all of us. Scarred her for life. In every sense. Every day I wake up and wish I could make

77

it all better for her – but I can't. And I blame myself for her accident."

"I blame myself for Smokey's death. I promised to look after him. I let him down." Jenni admitted.

"Then we have a lot in common," said Holly, her voice heavy with sorrow.

They sipped their sodas in silence for awhile, each reflecting on events of the past.

All of a sudden, Jenni found herself saying, "I should really go."

Holly glanced at the station clock. "What will you do for the rest of the day?"

Jenni shrugged. "I don't know. Go home I suppose. I might go for a walk first, now that the rain has stopped."

"Good idea."

"Holly."

"What?"

"Thank you."

"For what?"

"For saving my life."

"But you said you weren't going to jump anyway," Holly reminded her, smiling.

Jenni smiled. "I'm glad you were there."

"Me too," replied Holly.

"Goodbye weirdo."

Holly laughed. "Takes one to know one."

Maybe it was because of her late start at work, but the rest of the day seemed to go faster than usual for Holly. She thought a lot about her encounter with Jenni. It felt in some ways as if she had found a kindred spirit, but she told herself that was probably just in her head. After all, if Jenni had wanted more than one conversation, they would have exchanged phone numbers and suggested meeting again. It seemed a shame, but that was it. At least she should feel good about having saved someone's life. And she wondered if she would spend the rest of her life trying to save other people, in an attempt to make up for what had happened to her sister.

Holly dozed on the train ride home, which was unusual for her. *Too much thinking*, she told herself, *is not good for you*. She wasn't even looking out for the horse on the balcony, but he was there again in front of her. Watching and waiting. Or could she have been dreaming? She glanced around at her fellow passengers, but they were all cocooned in their own worlds, engrossed in a newspaper or magazine, or just thinking about what they would have for dinner that night. No one else seemed to have noticed the horse, or if they did, there was no evidence of it.

The house seemed very quiet when Holly returned, and

to her surprise the front door was locked. Claire should have been there. She felt fear in the pit of her stomach.

"Claire," she called, glancing into the living room, and then the kitchen. "Claire?"

Panic rising, she ran up the stairs and pushed open Claire's bedroom door. The room was empty. Claire's comforter was in its usual heap, and socks and clothes heaped on a chair, as always. "Claire, where are you?"

Visions of their father returning, distraught again. The blame, the guilt escalating, visions of the police, of newspaper headlines, "Missing girl." *You have to calm down*, she told herself. *Claire wouldn't do this to us again, not after last night.* Or would she? How much did she really know her sister? Where had she gone last night when she disappeared and why wouldn't she tell anyone?

"Claire!" she screamed.

Then she heard a car pull into the driveway. Their father was home and she prepared herself for the worst.

He was whistling when he came into the kitchen, sounding surprisingly cheerful. Why was she *always* the cause of unhappiness for him?

"Dad," she began slowly, wondering how to break it to him that his favorite daughter was missing again, when Claire appeared in the doorway.

Noticing the puzzled look on Holly's face, her father said, "Oh, by the way, I took Claire to work with me after

80

I came home at lunchtime. Thought it would be a good idea for both of us, and my boss was okay about it. Sorry, I should have left a note. You weren't worried were you?"

"Well, actually –" Holly started.

"I had a fun time helping Dad," said Claire. "I'm going tomorrow too!"

"Great," replied Holly.

"She did really well," commented their father when Claire had gone upstairs to change. "I think it's a positive step, don't you?"

"Absolutely," agreed Holly, not wanting to admit to herself how excluded she felt.

"Did you have a nice day shopping?" asked Jenni's mom when she got back. "You're home earlier than I expected."

"Problems on the train," Jenni replied. "So I had a soda and went for a walk instead, once the rain stopped."

Jenni had walked for a long time, back from the station and then up by the woods. She still clung to a glimmer of hope that Smokey would be there, but deep down she knew he wouldn't. Somehow, she had to come to terms with what had happened at the station. Would Smokey have appeared if Holly had not been there to save her? She would never know the answer. Unless she went back to the station and tried again.

"Oh. Is everything okay?"

"Fine, Mom. Don't worry."

Jenni made a decision. "I think I'm going into town again tomorrow," she announced to her mother.

"Okay, hon!"

Jenni replied, "I'm hoping the trains will be back to normal then. There's something I have to do."

Holly was surprised but pleased when Jenni turned up at the bookstore the following day.

"I didn't expect to see you again, *weirdo*. Haven't tried to jump off any more platforms lately, have you?"

Jenni smiled wryly and asked, "I wondered if you wanted company on your lunch break?"

"Okay. Here or somewhere else in town?" Holly wanted to know.

"Here is fine."

Half an hour later, Holly found herself telling Jenni about the horse on the balcony.

"Now you're thinking I'm as nutty as you," Holly joked.

Jenni shook her head. "Well, your story doesn't quite beat seeing a ghost horse, does it? Anyway, you've seen him more than once. I agree it sounds odd. It's not the kind of place you expect to see a horse."

"I know. That's why I haven't mentioned it to anyone else."

"So, what do you want to do about this mystery horse?" asked Jenni.

"Tell someone, and now I have," answered Holly.

"Let's go and find him."

"Are you serious?"

"Why not?" asked Jenni.

"It's not the normal thing to do."

"Hey, who said we were 'normal'?" replied Jenni.

"So where do we start?"

"I'll meet you here after work. We get on the train and you point out where you saw him. Who knows, maybe I'll see him too." Jenni was more than a little intrigued by Holly's story.

When Holly finished work that day, she wondered if Jenni would actually show up as planned, but when Holly got outside there she was, waiting outside the store. The train was full, but they managed to find a couple of empty seats next to each other.

"It was over there," said Holly, craning her neck as the train slowed down at the station that was the halfway point on her journey home.

Jenni followed her gaze. "Can you see him?"

Holly shook her head. "No. But he was standing on the balcony in that block of apartments."

"So we'd better get off at the next station then," suggested Jenni. "Let's see if we can find him."

83

Holly felt a flutter in her stomach as they made their way down the train and disembarked at an unfamiliar station. She didn't know if it was excitement or anxiety she felt, or both.

"So where do we start? It all looks so different now that we're not on the train."

Both girls felt disoriented. The view was not the same at all, now that they were on foot. "We need to look for landmarks," said Jenni. "What did you notice that was nearby?"

"Nothing in particular. This is crazy. This'll be like looking for a needle in a haystack!" Holly realized aloud.

"You can't give up before we even start," joked Jenni. "What about the apartments, for a start. They were high-rise, towering above other buildings. So we look upwards for tall buildings."

"That makes sense," agreed Holly, trying to keep calm as they both stared into the sky.

"Over there," said Jenni. "That's the block of apartments. We'll just keep walking in that direction."

"It could be miles."

"Yes. It could be," agreed Jenni.

They set off down a network of crisscrossing streets, away from the busy town center. After half an hour, it felt as if they had walked for miles and the tower block didn't seem any closer.

"Can you remember which way we came?" Holly asked Jenni. "We could easily get lost, if we aren't already."

"We can always ask somebody," replied Jenni. "Anyway it can't be much farther."

They continued to trudge through the streets, crossing over busy roads and dodging the commuter traffic and noise, until Holly said, "It feels like we've been walking around in a circle. I'm sure we've been down his road before."

"You could be right," replied Jenni. "Wait here." She stopped at a nearby newsstand and then returned smiling.

"I got some directions to the apartments. Next right, then two lefts, then cross the road and then we should be there. You got that?"

Holly's memory was not very efficient at the best of times. She liked to write everything down before she forgot it, but, encouraged, Jenni was already forging ahead.

As they were heading away from the town, the light was beginning to fade. Holly didn't feel comfortable with the area they were in. The buildings looked run down, the walls were covered in graffiti, and the local shops had iron bars on the windows. Her father would have told her this was not a good area to be in, especially for two girls on their own with night approaching. She was about to say, "I think we should turn back," when Jenni exclaimed, "That must be it. There! That block of apartments. Over there."

But as Holly followed her gaze, her relief turned to dismay. "But which block of apartments?"

Four decaying tower blocks confronted them.

"It only looked like one from the train!" Holly exclaimed in frustration.

"That's because they're in a row, one behind the other. So they're hidden from view from the train window."

"What do we do now?"

"We have to try them all," said Jenni.

"What if this isn't the right area at all?" ventured Holly, who was rapidly losing courage under the sporadic glow of the vandalized streetlights.

"It must be. It's this block of apartments, isn't it?"

"Well, it's *a* block of apartments," replied Holly. "What if there are lots of other rows of tower blocks and we're miles out in the wrong direction?"

"You saw it from the train, right?" Jenni reminded her new friend.

"I saw one from the train. Not these others. What if I made a mistake? What if we walked in a totally wrong direction? I don't like it here," Holly confessed.

"We've come this far, so we should at least look."

"It's too dark to see anything," Holly whined.

Jenni sensed this would be a losing battle and she

didn't want to investigate the area all by herself so she gave in. "Okay. Maybe we should come back and try again tomorrow."

It was frustrating to have hopes raised and then dashed. "At least we know where to come now, and it will be easier when it's light out."

They only had to ask one local shop for directions to get back to the station. It had definitely been a strange day.

As they waited on the platform for the train to come in, Holly got a text message from her Dad.

"Everything all right?" asked Jenni, sensing that Holly was feeling sad.

"Fine, thanks. Dad's taking Claire to the movies tonight, so they'll be back later."

As they sat down on the train Jenni said, "Why don't you come back to my house? We can have a bite to eat."

Holly was taken aback. "I'm not scared to go home to an empty house, if that's what you were thinking," she responded, a little defensively.

"I'd like you to come to mine. That's why I asked," said Jenni. "And you don't need to worry about getting back later. My Mom can bring you home. I'm sure she won't mind."

"Well, if you're really sure."

"Of course I am. I'm hungry after our wild goose chase."

"Me too."

"Good. That's settled then."

Jenni's mom was delighted when her daughter brought a new friend home. Holly was made to feel so welcome she was a little overwhelmed. It was very clear that Jenni's parents loved her very much and Holly found herself feeling envious.

When it was time to go home, Jenni's mom offered to drive her back, just as Jenni had predicted. How lucky Jenni was to be part of such a caring family. When they reached her house Holly said, "Thank you very much for having me over."

"It was our pleasure," Jenni's mom replied. She hadn't seen her daughter so animated for a long time, which she chalked up to Holly's company. "You are welcome any time."

"See you tomorrow then, Jenni?" Holly said as she opened the car door. The lights were on in the house and the car was in the drive, so she knew her Dad and Claire were home.

"Okay. See you tomorrow!"

Holly watched them drive away and was engulfed by a wave of sadness.

Chapter 8

The next day Holly received a text message from Jenni saying, *"Having second thoughts about meeting. Will be in touch."*

So that's it, she thought. A brief friendship, but it was fun while it lasted. Fun – what a novelty. At least her Dad and Claire had seemed in high spirits the previous night, and she was glad Claire was happier. They had chatted about the movie, which had been a comedy, and Holly wished she had been there with them. She couldn't remember the last time she had seen a movie in a theater. But then, if she had gone she wouldn't have met Jenni's parents, and she had really enjoyed her evening with a normal family.

The day at work dragged and she was lost in her own thoughts on the train ride home, listening to the train's rhythmic clatter. The rain poured down, making visibility poor, so even if the horse had been there, she would not have seen him. Besides, a horse wouldn't be out on a balcony in the rain. She almost laughed at the absurdity of it. Who would keep a horse on a balcony in the first place? She didn't hear the beep of a text coming though until the train stopped. It was Jenni. *"Too dark to search after work. Let's meet Sunday? Whole day then."*

Her heart lightened. Maybe they would be sharing another adventure after all.

Jenni had been wondering if the search for the horse on the balcony was fruitless, until she had another dream. She still often dreamed about riding Smokey again, and these dreams were bittersweet and left her waking up with a reinforced sense of loss and sadness. But this one was different. This time she was riding through town, with traffic on all sides, and she had been afraid but Smokey was unfazed and seemed to be cantering with a sense of purpose. "What's wrong, Smokey?" she had asked, but he broke into a gallop, as if in a hurry to get somewhere. Suddenly they were at the foot of a tall building and she was sure she could hear another horse calling to them. She looked up to the balcony and heard the other horse again. Smokey called back and then she woke up with a start, and an uneasy feeling in the pit of her stomach.

Although she told herself it was just a dream, for the rest of the day Jenni couldn't shake the feeling of unease. Maybe Smokey was trying to communicate with her again? Somehow, she and Holly had to find that mystery horse. Anxiously, she sent a text to Holly to make sure their Sunday search was still on.

Sunday was a long time coming, it seemed to Holly. But finally, she and Jenni were together again, walking the somewhat familiar route to the tower blocks. It wasn't as intimidating on a Sunday morning, with no commuter traffic, people rushing around or shadowy streetlights. The sun was shining for a start, and they had the whole day to search if they wanted.

"I'm still not convinced this is the right block of apartments," admitted Holly as they approached the area.

"There's only one way to find out, and that's to walk around all of them and see if there's a horse on the balcony," smiled Jenni. She had not yet mentioned the dream to Holly, deciding to keep it to herself for the time being.

"They're so run-down," commented Holly as they got nearer. "Are you sure people live here? I don't see many signs of life."

"And the windows are all boarded up over here," said Jenni.

But even so, they patrolled each of the four blocks, studying those with balconies for any sign of a horse. In some cases the balconies were crumbling away.

"This is hopeless," said Holly after a while. "We must have the wrong place. It just feels wrong."

"Maybe we should ask someone. After all, the locals would know if anyone keeps a horse here," suggested Jenni, who was not about to give up.

"What locals?" observed Holly. "Haven't you noticed how quiet it is around here? It's deserted, actually."

"Well, we've checked thoroughly, so maybe you're right and this isn't the same block you saw from the train. Want to take a break and find somewhere to grab a juice? I'm thirsty."

"Then we'll have to backtrack to where the shops are, because there's nothing around here." Holly felt defeated. What were they doing here?

"I think there was a café on the corner a few streets back," remarked Jenni.

The café looked as neglected as the rest of the area, with only one other customer, a scruffy looking young guy about their own age, pale and dark-haired, who was gnawing on a greasy hamburger with surprising enthusiasm.

Sitting by the window drinking juice, Holly said, "We're not going to find my mystery horse, are we?"

"Hey, don't give up yet. We have plenty of time to keep looking."

"But where?"

Before Jenni could respond a loud argument broke out between the burger-eating boy and the café owner.

"You're not conning me this time. I want payment now – or else."

"You'll get your money. I'll bring it in later," the boy replied.

"That's what you said last time, so now you owe me for two meals!"

"Hey, I wouldn't call this tasteless bun with mystery meat a meal," the boy said with attitude.

"The money. Now. Or I call the police."

"Don't be ridiculous." The boy got up to go, but the café owner, who was a burly, overweight man, grabbed his arm.

"Get off me!"

"Pay up," the café owner demanded.

"I don't have it."

"Then I'm calling the police."

Seeing the fear in the boy's eyes, Holly found herself saying, "How much do you owe?"

The boy seemed too astonished to reply, but the owner barked, "A five will cover the hassle he's causing me."

"Is that all?" Holly produced the money and thrust it at the owner.

"You must be crazy," he replied snatching it from her. "Either that or you like this idler. He's just a waste of space."

With that he pushed the boy toward the door, banging his leg into the table in the process.

"Hey, there's no need for that," said Holly. "Leave him alone!"

"Do you want a fight too then? Or maybe you know him? Maybe this is a set-up and you're planning to rob me – is that it?"

"Now you're the one who's crazy," retorted Holly boldly.

"Don't bait him," advised the boy. "He's got a nasty temper. We'd better get out of here before he loses it."

"I think he's right," said Jenni, grabbing her jacket, and the three of them made a beeline for the door before things got out of hand.

Once they were safely two streets away the boy said, "Thanks for helping."

"No problem," said Holly.

"She likes saving people," added Jenni. "It's her hobby."

"Are you from around here?" asked Holly.

"What's it to you?" replied the boy, suddenly defensive again. "I can see *you* aren't."

"Maybe you can help us," said Holly. "We're looking for something. We thought we might see it over at the tower block."

"Looking for what?" he asked suspiciously.

"A horse."

The boy gave her a curious stare. "Are you kidding?"

"No. We think… I thought… that I saw a horse there."

"That's not very likely, is it?" said the boy.

"Not really. But we won't stop looking until we find it."

Then, to their surprise, the boy said, "Well, I'm afraid you wasted a trip. There *was* a horse here. But not any longer."

Jenni's mouth dropped open and Holly was also astonished.

"*Was* a horse?"

"Yes, some idiot tried to keep one in that block of apartments that you mentioned, but it got reported and the authorities took it away."

"How do you know?"

"I used to live there. They're all boarded up now,

going to be demolished. The whole area is about to be re-developed. Well, I'd better get going. Lucky you bumped into me. It saved you wasting any more time on a pointless search."

"I suppose so."

"Thanks again for bailing me out in the café."

"Well, that's that then," said Holly when the boy had gone. "At least I know I didn't imagine the horse."

But something about the situation didn't feel quite right to Jenni. "Let's just hope the horse is being looked after properly now."

They walked back to the station, feeling subdued. After awhile Holly said, "How would you like to come back to my house?"

When they got off the train at Holly's stop, she wondered if it had been a good idea to bring Jenni home. She had texted Claire to tell her she was bringing a friend back, so Claire could decide whether or not to be there. Their Dad would still be at work, so it wouldn't exactly be like the family meal she has shared at Jenni's place.

But Claire did not text back.

"I'm not sure if my sister will be there or not, since she's shy of strangers," explained Holly. "If you get to meet her, you'll see why."

But the house was empty, so Holly made some iced

tea and the two girls sat in the kitchen chatting. It felt good and Holly was relieved that Claire wasn't there. Her relief was rapidly followed by the usual feelings of guilt. Then she heard the door and before she realized it, Claire had stopped short in the kitchen doorway.

"Oh. I didn't know we had visitors."

"I texted you."

"My phone's in the charger upstairs."

"Sorry," Holly felt totally wrong footed. "This is Jenni."

"Hi, Jenni," said Claire awkwardly.

"Hello, Claire," Jenni replied, hoping that she had successfully disguised the shock she was feeling on being confronted with the terrible scars on the girl's face. But Claire, used to people's embarrassed reactions to her appearance, had noticed immediately.

"Do you want an iced tea?" offered Holly anxiously.

"No thanks. I've got things to do. See you later." And with that she turned and made a hasty retreat upstairs to her room.

"I should have warned you. I'm sorry," muttered Holly.

"Hey, what do you have to be sorry for?" replied Jenni.

"Everything," said Holly under her breath.

"I should be apologizing to Claire. I hope I haven't upset her. I just wasn't expecting… it was rude of me to stare. I didn't mean to."

And suddenly the relaxed atmosphere between them

had gone, replaced by mutual awkwardness until Jenni said, inevitably, "I really ought to be going now."

Monday morning came and went and Holly had plenty of time on her train journey to reflect on recent events. Something about the boy did not feel right to her, but she felt she had no choice but to accept what he had told them. Even so, she was surprised to see the horse again on her way home. There he was – the horse on the balcony! This time she wasn't going to give up so easily. She got off at the next stop and set off for the block of apartments, running until her legs were aching. And there was the horse, miles above her, his golden head leaning on the railings, gazing out across the town below. She grabbed her phone and called Jenni's number.

Chapter 9

It felt like forever, but finally Jenni joined Holly at the apartments, by which time the horse had disappeared again.

"I know you might think I'm making it up, but the *horse was there*," insisted Holly. "And this time I have proof!"

She handed her phone to Jenni. "I took some pics. But if these apartments are about to be demolished, this isn't a safe place for a horse to be. We have to get him out. And fast!"

Suddenly, Jenni's dream made sense and she had a bad feeling about the building. "I couldn't agree more," she said. "Let's go."

It didn't take long to find the stairs. "It's a long walk. I counted the levels and he was at least halfway up the building," said Holly.

Many flights and much panting later, the girls finally reached the floor that Holly felt sure was where the horse was located.

"But which door? There are so many."

"We'll knock on all of them," replied Jenni. "We have to find him."

The corridor was soon echoing with the sound of fists banging on wood. "No one lives here," said Holly as their efforts were met with silence.

"Well, someone does, because that horse didn't get here by himself," remarked Jenni. Suddenly, they heard the sound of a door opening at the end of the corridor, and a boy's head peered furtively out.

Holly and Jenni stared at each other as they recognized him.

"You're the boy from the café, aren't you?" asked Jenni, amazed at the coincidence.

The boy shrugged. "Dunno what you mean."

"You must remember," persisted Jenni. "My friend paid your bill. We were asking about a horse."

"No." He looked sullen, almost evasive.

"Well, I recognize *you*," continued Jenni. "I thought you said these apartments were condemned?"

"They are. So you should get out."

But at that moment there was the unmistakable sound of a soft whicker.

"You have that horse here, don't you?" exclaimed Holly. "I knew it!"

The boy tried to push the door shut but Holly was too quick and stuck her foot in the way and then her whole body. With the combined weight of Jenni and Holly, the girls barged inside, despite the boy's efforts to stop them. And there he was, at last, standing right before them. The mystery horse. He was stunning; a golden palomino with silvery mane and tail, and a dished face with big brown eyes that considered them with gentle curiosity.

Jenni gazed in awe. Up until now, she had half wondered if Holly had indeed imagined the horse she had described, since she herself had never seen it and it sounded so bizarre. Ironic, she thought, because Ella would have said the same about her seeing Smokey. But now she knew this horse was real. *Very* real.

"He's so beautiful," said Holly.

"Get out. Both of you," repeated the boy, more scared than angry. "You're trespassing."

"I doubt it. I bet you're the one who shouldn't be

here," retorted Holly. "Why did you lie to us? You said the horse had been taken away."

"I had to lie. To get rid of you. You shouldn't be here."

"Did you steal the horse?" demanded Jenni.

"Go away. Leave us alone."

"Maybe we should call the police," threatened Holly. "I mean, it's not a normal thing, keeping a horse in a place like this. Cruel, I'd say."

"The horse is mine. He belongs to me," the boy insisted.

"I don't believe you," Holly answered.

"Why should I care what you think? Now, get out!"

Jenni looked at their surroundings and for a moment she wondered if the boy was telling the truth. The place was a studio, she guessed, a large room that once would have had a kitchen area, sofa bed, and a bathroom. A home for someone. But all that was left was a shell. Bare floorboards, tattered curtains, a grubby sleeping bag for the boy, old pizza cartons. There was no furniture. There was only a tiny camping stove. The boy looked unkempt, unwashed, and scruffy. The horse, by contrast, was groomed, with a shiny coat, clean water bucket, and bale of good hay.

"Is he really your horse?" she asked.

"I told you he is, didn't I?"

"How long have you been living here?"

"Squatting, more like," said Holly.

"Too long," replied the boy, and he sounded tired.

"The place looks like it should be torn down," said Holly.

"It will be," replied the boy, his face drawn and pale.

"Maybe we can help you," said Jenni.

"Why would you want to do that?" asked the boy suspiciously. "Anyway, I thought you were all set to call the police."

"Do you live here alone?" asked Jenni.

"No. I live here with Samurai." And hearing his name, the horse ambled over to the boy and rested his head on the boy's shoulder, blowing softly on his tousled hair. Jenni felt her heartstrings tug as she recalled how Smokey used to do that with her. At that moment she knew the boy was telling the truth.

"Let us help you," she said. "I'm Jenni. And this is Holly."

"I'm Seth," muttered the boy.

"How on earth did you get Samurai up here?" wondered Holly in amazement. "All those steps."

"The service elevator still works. Just," he said. "At night, when it's dark, I take Samurai down in the elevator and then we go for a walk behind the apartments, over to the only patch of green grass for miles, so he can graze and wander."

"That must be tricky."

"Just a bit," said the boy, managing the hint of a smile. "It's scary, wondering if the elevator will break down and hoping no one will see us. I shouldn't be here. The place has been condemned, but up until last week there was another group of squatters on the first floor. They were okay though; they left us alone. But even they realized it was time to get out. It's just not safe here."

"Then you have to get out."

"Do you think I don't know that? I have nowhere else to go," replied the boy.

"So how did you end up here?" wondered Jenni.

"I used to be with a circus. I was a trick rider with Samurai. He's brilliant." He patted the horse, which was still nuzzling his hair. "But the audiences got smaller and smaller, and in the end, the circus owner knew we had to close down for good. So that was it. I'm out of a job, and out of a home. A lot of the animals were sold or put down, but I couldn't lose Samurai. He's my best friend."

"What about your family?"

"I never knew my Mom. My Dad, well, he got desperate when the circus closed. I mean, how likely are you to find work as a trapeze artist? He got in with some bad people and ended up in prison."

"That's awful!" Jenni said. "So who took care of you?"

"My older brother, Luka. He's always looked out for

me. He got work on a building site and we rented a trailer to live in so we could still keep Samurai. It was tough, but we managed. Then the work ran out and we lost the trailer. Luka knew some people who were squatting here so we moved in. We only planned to stay a few days. After all, it's not the best place to keep a horse. But we needed somewhere just until Luka could get another job. But one night, a few weeks ago, Luka went out and never came back."

"Any idea where he could have gone?" wondered Holly.

Seth shook his head. "Not a clue. And he wouldn't have deserted me, if that's what you're thinking. Not Luka."

"Have you reported him missing?" asked Jenni.

"I can't go to the police, because I'd be taken into custody and then I'd lose Samurai and I couldn't bear that. He's all I've got left in the world."

Poor Seth, thought Jenni. *We have to help him.*

"I've told you too much," said Seth. "Now it's your turn. What are you doing here and why are you so interested in my horse?"

Suddenly Samurai jerked his head abruptly, his ears twitching, his breathing agitated.

"What's wrong, boy?" Seth wondered anxiously.

Then they all felt the tremor.

105

"What was that?" said Holly.

"It was like the floor sort of wobbled," said Jenni nervously.

"We have to get out of here – and fast," exclaimed Seth, grabbing Samurai's head collar.

Holly scooped up Seth's backpack, which she guessed contained everything he owned in the world, just as the walls began to shake. The fear in her voice was audible. "It's falling in, isn't it?"

At that moment, there was a cracking sound and a huge lump of plaster dropped from the ceiling, almost landing on Samurai's back. Alarmed, he reared up, narrowly missing Seth's arms with his hooves. Even a calm horse like Samurai was spooked by something this scary.

"The building is crumbling!" said Seth.

They all rushed for the door at once, but Samurai refused to budge.

"He's terrified. We have to stay calm," advised Seth. "We have to pretend everything is okay so he trusts us."

"But everything isn't okay," said Holly.

"We have to pretend. We have to convince Samurai we're not going to panic." He stroked the horse's muzzle, saying in soothing tones, "It's alright, boy, nothing to worry about. You're safe with us."

At first, Samurai continued to dig his heels in but eventually he started to relax enough to allow Seth to coax him forward. Then they were out of the door and in the gloomy corridor with graffiti covered walls.

"We can't risk using the service elevator," advised Holly.

"So how are we going to get Samurai out? We're on the sixth floor!"

"We'll have to use the stairs."

"Will Samurai be able to manage that?"

"We've done it before, when we had to."

So they descended the first flight of stairs with Samurai carefully making his way down. They all prayed that nothing else would spook him before they got out. Suddenly, there was another loud crash above their heads and Samurai started to shake.

"What was that?" Holly said out loud.

"I don't want to think about it," replied Seth. "This is just too dangerous."

"And no one knows we're here," said Jenni. "What if we get trapped?"

The same thoughts occurred to Holly and Seth. It was slow and perilous, but somehow they managed to get down the next five flights of stairs. Holly was amazed at Samurai's bravery.

"One more to go," gasped Jenni as they turned the corner, but they were unprepared for what met their horrified faces.

"The stairwell collapsed," said a stunned Holly. "It's just a gaping hole!"

"There must be a fire escape," said Jenni. "Seth, tell me there's a fire escape."

"Yes. But we have to go back along the corridor. Some stairs are outside, from the balcony. "If they're still intact."

Holly prayed as she had never prayed before. But when they saw the emergency stairs their faces fell.

"Spiral stairs. Far too narrow for a horse. How on earth are we going to get Samurai down?"

"You girls get out while you can," said Seth. "I have to stay here with Samurai."

"Don't be stupid. We're not leaving you," retorted Jenni. "There must be a way out for Samurai!"

"There is," said Holly, her stomach churning at the thought. "He'll have to jump."

"You're kidding. That's crazy!"

"Maybe not," said Seth. "It's about seven feet down. He can jump. He used to jump through giant hoops of fire in the circus."

"Then you'll have to go down first, Seth, and call him to you. He won't come to us," said Holly. At first Seth was reluctant but there was no time to debate it.

"I'll stay up here with Samurai and keep him calm," offered Jenni.

So Seth and Holly made their way down the spiral stairs, jumped into the gaping hole and waited on the ground. Seth called frantically and tried to coax his horse down while Jenni tried to soothe Samurai, hoping there would be no more falling debris.

"It's no use," said Seth desperately. "He won't come to me. I'm going back up."

Suddenly, there was a tremendous crash and they noticed the bolts that secured the emergency stairs were starting to come loose. Jenni quickly realized that Samurai wasn't the only one trapped now. Visions of her brother, Az, and the rock climbing birthday surprise flooded back. She had never managed to overcome her fear of heights, but she couldn't afford to panic. Not now.

"We have to get help!" screamed Holly.

"They'll never get here in time," groaned Seth. "That floor's going to collapse. Samurai has to jump. *With* Jenni!"

"Come on, boy, or we'll both be killed," Jenni urged the frightened horse, who teetered on the edge, looking down at the grass below. For a moment she was back on the rock face, trembling in her safety harness as she stared at the boulders below. She remembered Az telling her it was easy and that she had to face her fears. He had gone first to show her it was safe, but there was no safety harness this time. Suddenly, Jenni became aware of another presence on the balcony. She heard a soft low whicker that did not come from Samurai.

"Smokey?" she gasped. She couldn't see him, but she knew he was there and so did Samurai, who whickered a response. Then there was a flash of gray as Smokey jumped onto the grass below, showing Samurai that it was safe to follow. In an instant, Jenni threw herself onto Samurai's back before he followed Smokey's cue and took an enormous leap. It felt as if they were flying, like in the dream she had before her encounter with Holly at the railway station. She closed her eyes, braced herself for the landing and hung on for dear life. When she opened them again, Samurai had hit the grass, momentarily thrown off balance. But then he recovered and stood stock still, as if stunned that he had survived.

"Thank goodness you're okay," said Holly "You are okay, aren't you?"

Jenni nodded, unable to catch her breath as she slid off Samurai's back, her legs trembling. As more rubble descended, they dashed across the road to safety.

"I didn't think he was going to jump, but he did. Good boy!" Seth hugged his beloved horse before hastily checking his legs for any signs of injury. Watching their faces, Jenni realized that neither Seth nor Holly had seen Smokey's ghost. Only she and Samurai had seen it.

She decided it should remain their secret. After all, who would believe her?

Still in shock, Holly looked at the rubble and then at Seth and said smiling, "Well, looks like you have to come with us now."

Chapter 10

"How are we going to get Samurai back to your place, Jenni?" wondered Holly. "It's much too far to walk." A brief discussion had established that Samurai would stay in Smokey's stable where he would be safe.

"Do you have a horse trailer?" asked Seth.

"No," replied Jenni, "but I know someone who does." She had not spoken to Ella for ages and now she had to ask for a favor. This could be awkward, but she couldn't think of anyone else to ask. She opened her cell phone and clicked on Ella's name in her address book. At first, it just called the number and Jenni wracked her brain wondering what to do if there was no reply. Finally, a voice said, "What do you want, Jenni?"

At least she hasn't deleted me from her address book, thought Jenni, relieved.

"Hi. You okay?" began Jenni awkwardly.

"Fine." Ella said curtly.

"I need to ask a favor."

This was met with silence.

"It's really important."

"I tried to be your friend, Jen, but you threw it back in my face."

"I know and I'm sorry. But I need your help right now."

"Go away. I'm busy."

"*Please* Ella, just hear me out." Jenni begged.

"Why should I?"

"Because it's an emergency and it involves a horse."

"A ghost horse or a real one?" Ella asked.

"He's very real. He's lost his home and needs a place to stay, so I'm taking him back to mine, but we're miles away. It's too far to walk. Can I borrow your trailer?"

"Are you messing with me, Jen?"

"No. This is serious." Jenni told her ex-friend.

113

"Where are you?"

Jenni gave her the name of the train station.

"Hey, you're a long way out. I'll have to ask Dad to drive me there. Lucky for you he's home and snoozing on the sofa."

"I'll be so grateful if he can help."

"I'll do my best," Ella replied.

"Thanks, Ella."

They arranged to meet at the station and Ella promised to call back if her Dad said no.

"We'd better make our way to the station. Fingers crossed that Ella's Dad will help us out," said Holly.

Samurai walked happily beside Seth as they set off together, and Jenni wondered what passersby must have thought. It wasn't the kind of place you expected to see a horse out for a stroll, but Samurai was calm and seemed unfazed by the traffic as they got closer to the station.

This got Holly thinking again about her sister, and what a horse like Samurai could do for her. While they waited for their ride, Jenni said, "I can make up a story about finding Samurai, but what about Seth?"

"What do you mean?" asked Holly.

"She means that her parents will want to know who I am and where I come from, and if I tell them then they will say they need to contact the authorities and I'll be taken away."

"Oh. I didn't think of that." But when she did, Holly realized that if she took Seth home, her Dad would ask all sorts of questions too.

"Well, there's no way I'm letting that happen," said Seth.

"So what do we do?" wondered Holly.

"Until we can work it out, Seth can hide in Smokey's old stable with Samurai. If that's okay with you, Seth?"

"I don't have many choices right now," replied Seth. "And whatever happens I want to make sure that Samurai is safe. Speaking of which, I never got a chance to find out why you were so interested in my horse in the first place."

"I think Holly should tell you that," said Jenni.

Holly smiled sadly. "It'll probably sound a little crazy to you, but it's because of my sister. She was badly burned in an accident when she was younger. It was my fault. I should have been watching her, but I didn't. She hides away in the house most of the time now, because of the way people react to her scars. She used to ride, and she was great with horses. They were her passion. But she's now convinced herself that even horses are afraid of her."

"So where do I come in?"

"I wanted to put things right. I thought if I could find a horse, the perfect horse – that will be her friend and trust

115

her and love her, restore her faith – then she might have a chance of living a normal life."

"You thought Samurai could do that? Why?"

"I figured a horse that's calm enough to live in a high-rise apartment without being fazed must be a special horse."

"Well, you're right about him being special," Seth replied.

"I can see a trailer," said Jenni suddenly. "I think our rescue party is here at last."

She wondered what it would feel like to be face to face with Ella again, and started feeling a little apprehensive. Ella was clearly surprised that Jenni was not alone with the horse.

"Hi, Ella. This is Seth and Holly. They've been helping me," she explained. "They're all coming back to my place."

"Right." Ella's voice was somewhat strained.

"Thank you so much," said Jenni gratefully as the ramp was lowered and Samurai trotted obediently into the trailer. He had traveled many times with the circus so he was used to it.

"So far so good," thought Holly. They all piled into the old trailer, and on the drive back they managed to field off any questions from Ella's Dad, who mercifully seemed to accept the behavior of horse-crazed teenagers. It felt strange for Jenni and Ella to be together again, and Holly could sense the tension between them. Seth gazed out of the window, thinking about his rather uncertain future. It was kind of Jenni to help, he mused, but this could only be a temporary arrangement. He would have to find somewhere else to live. And what about Samurai's future?

Eventually, a familiar field and stable came into view, and for the first time in ages Jenni was glad to be back home. Seth unloaded Samurai, who sniffed the air curiously with his ears flicking back and forth at this new environment. They all thanked Ella and her Dad profusely and then waved goodbye to them, having much to do.

Ella offered them straw for the stable and hay for the feed net until they could get everything sorted out. Jenni battled with her mixed emotions as she and Holly prepared Smokey's empty stable for the new resident. She could be sad later, she told herself. They had to make sure Samurai would be comfortable for the night before it got too dark.

Seth led Samurai around the perimeter of the field, letting him explore his unfamiliar environment, while Dylan watched from over his stable door with great interest. Finally, everything was ready and Samurai ventured into his new home. They all watched with delight as he snuffled the fresh straw and then ducked hungrily into the well-stuffed hay net.

"Someone's happy," said Seth, relieved.

"I should be getting home," said Holly.

"I'll get Mom to take you," offered Jenni.

"Thanks so much, you two," said Seth.

"Well, it's certainly been an interesting Sunday," replied Jenni.

Later, when her parents were watching TV, Jenni smuggled food, juice and a sleeping bag out of the house and took it across to the field for Seth. Samurai was leaning his head over the half door, dozing, and it felt so odd to Jenni to see another horse in Smokey's stable. But, to her surprise, she was okay with it somehow.

The next morning, Jenni woke up early and actually felt excited about the day ahead. After showering and dressing, she practically skipped across to the field. Seth was already up and sitting outside the stable, soaking up the sun.

"I brought us orange juice, croissants and cheese," she said. "We can have a picnic. Oh, and tea for later."

"Sounds good to me," said Seth appreciatively.

"Did Samurai settle in alright last night?"

"Sure did. This must feel like a luxury hotel to him," joked Seth, adding, "and me."

"My parents are happy for him to stay as long as you want." Jenni had overheard her mom before she came out, telling her Dad how pleased she was that their daughter seemed to have a new focus, and how good it was for her to have met Holly and to have another horse to care for. "Do you need anything else for him, like brushes or a hoof pick?"

"Thanks, but I have those in my backpack. I thought I would let Samurai out, now that he's had a chance to get used to being here. What do you think?"

"Great idea."

Seth slid back the bolts on the stable door and Samurai stepped into the morning air, tentatively at first. He looked at Seth as if waiting for approval, and then carefully set off around the field, investigating cautiously. Finally, satisfied that all was well, he gave a joyful whinny, kicked up his heels and broke into a gallop. It was a wonderful sight.

"He probably can't remember seeing so much green grass," observed Seth. "I wanted to wait until you were here, to share this with us."

Watching Samurai, Jenni felt tears welling up in her eyes. Seth discreetly looked away.

"Holly told me about Smokey. You must have loved him very much." Seth said.

"More than words can say," she replied, her voice choked with emotion.

"I know. Samurai means the world to me."

They sat with their own private thoughts for a while until Samurai trotted over and tossed his head playfully, as if to say, "Come on you two, cheer up!"

"It's good to see him running free. Not the right place for a horse, in a high-rise block of apartments," said Seth. "I'm so glad you and Holly found me. At just the right time, too." He paused, as if deep in thought. "Would you like to ride Samurai?"

Jenni was taken aback. "Really?"

Seth nodded. "Actually, I think you should. So does Samurai."

Before she could reply, he attached a rope to the head collar. "Do you need a leg up?"

And before she knew it, she grabbed her helmet and Jenni was riding again! Samurai was a truly amazing horse. He was strong and powerful, yet gentle and good-natured. Any anxieties she might have had were soon dispelled as they trotted and then cantered across the field. She leaned forward and buried her face in his silver mane, breathing in his wonderful horsey smell and feeling the softness of his silky coat against her face. She was transported to heaven. When she returned to where Seth was waiting, her eyes were wet once more.

"You're not crying again, are you? I don't *do* tears," teased Seth.

"Of joy," she replied. Not only had she experienced a

truly breathtaking ride, but she no longer felt guilty that she was somehow betraying Smokey's memory. It was a liberating feeling. "Can I just take him around the field one more time?" Jenni asked.

"Be my guest."

This time when she rode back to the stable, there was a visitor waiting.

"I certainly never expected to see you ride again," said Ella, adding, "Good for you, Jen."

"Hi Ella. Thanks again for helping us. We owe you big time!"

"Too right," joked Ella. "And you can start by helping me muck out Dylan's stall."

"Maybe it's time the two horses got to know each other better," suggested Seth, adding, "Who knows, they may become best friends."

Ella and Jenni exchanged knowing glances and then they watched while Dylan was turned out with Samurai. Curiosity and caution was followed by play fighting, and then the horses chased each other around the field, finally settling under the tree together where they began a mutual grooming session.

"Well, I think it's safe to say they like each other," laughed Ella. "In fact, Dylan is probably very glad to have company again. He gets lonely on his own."

✣ ✣ ✣ ✣ ✣

Holly had spent all day in the bookstore, clock watching. She just wanted to finish work so she could go over to see Jenni and Seth and Samurai. When she had gotten home the previous night, she told Claire all about Samurai and what a fantastic horse he was, trying to persuade her sister to join her to meet him, but to her disappointment, Claire refused. It was so frustrating. Traveling back on the train, it felt odd, gazing through the window and knowing she would never see that horse on the balcony again. But how could she get Claire to meet Samurai?

Later, Holly arrived at the stable and Jenni explained the situation to her and Seth. Jenni wondered, "Why do you think she won't come?"

"Hmm, she's already met me," Holly added.

"Only briefly. You're still a stranger to her, and she's so nervous with strangers."

"The solution is simple," said Seth. "We take Samurai to her."

"What a great idea! When?"

"How about now? Why waste time?" Seth answered.

It took them an hour, with Seth and Jenni taking turns riding Samurai, and when they reached Holly's house she said, "I should have called Claire first, to warn her we were coming."

"From what you've said, I think she would have made

sure she *wasn't* around when we got here if you'd done that," observed Seth.

But Claire had seen them from the window, because as they came up to the door, she appeared, saying in an agitated voice, "I *told* you last night Holly, I don't want to *see* anyone." But before she could run away, her eyes fell upon Samurai and in an instant she melted. "What a beautiful horse..."

"I told you, didn't I?" replied Holly. "Come and say hello to him."

Claire stretched her hand out and Samurai gently grazed her upturned palm with his lips. She smiled. "It tickles."

Jenni still felt uncomfortable seeing Claire's scarred face, but Seth appeared completely unfazed by it, almost as if he didn't notice, saying, "Hi, Claire. I'm Seth and this is Samurai and he's been wanting to meet you."

Holly also noticed Seth's reaction to Claire and the way she was falling in love with Samurai. "I'm hot after all that walking," she said. "Anyone want a drink?"

"Something cold would be great," said Seth.

"I'll get some water for Samurai," offered Jenni.

When they had disappeared into the house, Seth said to Claire, "You are lucky to have a sister like Holly. She thinks the world of you."

"I know," replied Claire, shyly meeting his gaze.

"I have a brother, Luka. Wish I knew where he was. I miss him so much."

"You must be worried sick. What happened?" Claire asked him.

Soon Claire found herself talking to this stranger as if she had known him for years, while they both fussed and stroked the stunning golden horse.

Holly watched from the window as the boy and girl talked earnestly. Then she saw them smiling and laughing.

"I think that Seth and Samurai are a gift from heaven," she said.

And when she came outside with a tray of cold drinks, Claire was sitting astride the golden palomino.

"Seth and I are going down by the field so I can ride Samurai properly. Is that okay?"

"That's fine, Claire. Enjoy it!" Holly said in shock.

When Claire and Seth returned, Claire still riding Samurai, she looked radiant. "This horse is incredible," she enthused. Holly had never seen her sister so happy.

When Seth, Samurai and Jenni had gone back home, all Claire could talk about was Samurai.

The next day, while Holly was sitting on the train on the way to work, a text message came through from Jenni.

It simply said, "Seth's gone." Holly felt sick to her stomach. How was she going to break the news to Claire? She knew she couldn't focus at work, not now. It was as if the gift of happiness that was handed to them had been snatched away again before they had time to enjoy it. On her ride home, she got off the train and walked to Jenni's house. Jenni was standing by the gate, gazing at two horses grazing contentedly. One was a golden palomino.

"But Samurai is still here. I thought…" Holly began, puzzled. "You said Seth was gone. Where? Why?"

"He left a note. Here." Jenni handed her friend a crumpled scrap of paper.

I know Samurai will be safe with you. He and Claire made a real connection. Seeing Claire and Holly together made me realize that I have to find Luka. I need my brother. Sorry to just go like this, but I hate goodbyes and I don't do tears. I hope one day I can come back again. Until then, thanks for everything.
  Seth.

Within a few weeks, a field was rented close to Claire's house and an overjoyed Claire became Samurai's new guardian. Holly was thrilled too, and their father couldn't have been happier, even though it would be a financial struggle to keep a horse. Holly offered to share the cost

125

of Samurai's keep with her wages, and even considered the possibility of riding him one day. Finally, the family's future looked brighter.

Standing alone by Smokey's now empty field, Jenni reflected on everything that had happened and decided to go for a walk by the river, which was once their favorite route. She sat for a while on the grass, watching a little kingfisher hunting. For a moment she still wanted to pretend that nothing had changed, that Smokey was behind her grazing contentedly. She closed her eyes and she could see Smokey again, but this time he was jumping from the balcony of the apartments, urging her to follow. He was telling her that this time she had to save herself. However scared she was, she had to face her fears and make that leap. Az had been right after all. Finally, Jenni was ready to jump.

Hearing the sound of hoofbeats she opened her eyes and looked up to see Ella and Dylan riding toward her. She grinned and waved. It was a pity that Dylan had lost his new stable companion so soon, she reflected. Maybe she should do something about that. She already had a copy of the local newspaper and scanned the Horses for Sale ads. There was one in particular that seemed like a strong possibility; a chestnut mare, eight years old, with a steady temperament, whose owner had outgrown her.

It wasn't far from home and was worth a visit. Maybe she would discuss it with Ella and Holly when they came around later on, to get their opinions.

She smiled. Maybe Seth had been right. Some things just happened at the right time and at the right place.